THE BONKERS BOOK OF JOBS!

MARK WILKINSON & JOHN AMBROSE

© Mark Wilkinson and John Ambrose 2018
Illustrations © Terry Cooper 2018

Published by
Candy Jar Books,
Mackintosh House
136 Newport Road, Cardiff, CF24 1DJ
www.candyjarbooks.co.uk

Edited by Shaun Russell & Will Rees

ISBN: 978-1-912535-00-2

Printed and bound in the UK by
4edge, 22 Eldon Way, Hockley, Essex, SS5 4AD

IntroDuction

Welcome to the Bonkers Book of Jobs
— containing the wackiest careers
in the world!

Just think, one day you'll spend a huge chunk of your life at work. What do you really want to do? Well, here is your chance to find out.

We have everything from the **SMELLIEST** jobs in the world to the scariest, from the MOST EVIL to the MOST DISGUSTING, from the funniest to the tastiest.

Have your teachers ever told you about these jobs?

- Dog food taster.
- Maggot farmer.
- Face feeler.

Of course they haven't. So, in this book, we will.

Lots of teachers avoid talking about some careers because they just don't understand them. They'll tell you that accountancy is a boring job, but fail to tell you that accountants can bring down gangsters!

This book will guide you through the ups and downs of work. As you progress through each of the chapters you will discover what the jobs involve, how much money you could earn, and how many of those jobs will be needed in the future.

At the end of each chapter we and **you** will rate how bonkers each job is in our crazyometer.

And at the end of the book the crazyometer will show you which bonkers jobs you could be doing in the future.

What job is...?

Disgusting...
Weird...
Scary...
Cool...
Delicious...
Or even stupid?

Ever thought about being a golf ball diver, dog yoga instructor or colour distribution technician? What's that? Read on...

Chapters

Disgusting Jobs

Let's face it, some jobs involve you doing disgusting things. You can't hide the fact, you can't dress it up, the tasks are nothing but **disgusting**.

But sometimes being **disgusting** is just the thing. It can give you that certain *je ne sais quoi* **(that's French for 'a certain something')** over your friends, and a halo of shame for them to admire. One person's **disgusting** is, after all, another person's SHOCK AND AWE.

DID YOU KNOW?

- A chiropodist treats verrucas and ingrown toenails and earns £27,000 a year.
- An arachnologist works with spiders and gets paid over £30,000 a year.

- A water treatment worker cleans up sewage in water and can earn up to £25,000 a year.

So don't rule out these careers – disgusting they may be, but that's 'disgusting + je ne sais quoi'.

MAGGOT FARMER

Maggots – marvellous creatures. They look creepy, feel wriggly and their life's purpose is to turn into flies. So, fancy a career that will see you breed them? Grow them? Feed them?

Why not? Just think of the practical jokes you could play on your friends. Like, how many maggots you can put down their pants.

How many insects are housed in giant cages in the world's largest commercial fly farm?

IS IT?

    a)   1 million.

    b)   100 million.

    c)   8.5 billion.

The answer is... C. That's a lot of maggots for practical jokes.

But why are all these maggots needed? Surely fishing hasn't got that popular? Well no. Maggots can be turned into animal feed or even diesel fuel.

It's cheaper than other animal feed, so we can farm more animals, increase the availability of cheap food and feed the ever increasing world population.

Fancy it? Then just take the same route that you would take into farming – maybe going to university to take a degree in something agricultural. After all, it's the same ideas as farming other animals, it just happens that these are disgusting.

BUT BE WARNED – what makes the job truly disgusting is the environment you'll be in. Giving billions of flies decaying rubbish to feed off – now just think of that stench! Pooey. OH AND WHEN DO YOU THINK THE FARM WILL BE OPEN?

    a)   9-5pm.
    b)   6-8pm.
    c)   24 hours a day.

The answer is c.

Trainee farmers earn £20k-ish, and if you end up managing the biggest maggot farms you will be on over £50k a year. Now that's not disgusting.

Bonkers Jobs Scorecard for Maggot Farmer

Now you've learned about the job it's time to score it. Below we have worked out a Crazyometer score for the job – do you agree? Just mark each aspect of the job out of 10. 1 meaning 'rubbish' and 10 meaning 'brilliant'. Then total up your score to see if you agree with the Crazyometer.

Aspect	Bonkers Jobs Score	Your Score
Are your friends impressed?	8 (They like me, being disgusting)	
Do your parents dislike it?	5 (They're not keen but the money is good)	
Do you earn much money?	7 (20k+ isn't bad)	
Nice place to work?	3 (No, but could be fun!)	
Job opportunities increasing?	9 (Yes)	
How brainy have you got to be?	6 (May have to go to university)	
Crazyometer Total Score	38	

Now keep reading and scoring the next disgusting job. At the end of the chapter we'll give you a chance to compare your scores of these jobs and choose one that shows off your bonkers side.

BEAUTICIAN

You may be surprised to see beautician in our list of disgusting jobs. But just think about it for a second. What are you working with? Bodies of **ALL** shapes and sizes!

And what are you doing to them? **PLUCKING**, **SCRAPING** and **waxing**!

Just because the name has beauty in it does not mean that what you do is beautiful. Your role here is to make something else beautiful – which means you'll be removing the rubbish.

And when I say rubbish, I mean all the rubbish both on the inside and out. They say that beauty is only skin deep, but one of the jobs of a beautician is to remove what is under the skin. Also, under the nails, in the teeth, and on the feet.

And even if you can put up with **disgustingly** smelly feet, then there's still one other treatment you might have to perform. **THE MOST DISGUSTING OF THEM ALL...**

Colonic irrigation doesn't sound that bad, until you realise that the 'colon' part of colonic refers to the part of your body that links the stomach to your bottom. Irrigation means 'washing out'. Put the two together and colonic irrigation = washing out a bottom. **Disgusting!**

Now the beautician doesn't sit there with a bowl and some soap and gloves, requesting that the client bend over. Instead the client lays on their side and the beautician inserts a tube into the rectum (bum) through which hot water is squirted to clean out the colon. Through the tube the loosened **POO** then flows from the client and into a bucket.

Guess who has to get rid of that?

Along with this disgusting speciality there are other potentially **disgusting** opportunities! Working with chemicals that can irritate the skin and eyes and working with dyes that can aggravate allergic reactions. **NICE!**

So how much do you get paid for performing these disgusting acts? Starting salaries are on average around £21k, and you'll need to have studied a beauty qualification or apprenticeship.

AND YOU KNOW WHAT. THE DEMAND FOR COLONIC IRRIGATION IS ON THE INCREASE!

Bonkers Jobs Scorecard for Beautician

Now you've learnt about the job it's time to score it. Below we have worked out a Crazyometer score for the job – do you agree? Just mark each aspect of the job out of 10, 1 meaning 'rubbish' and 10 meaning 'brilliant'. Then total up your score to see if you agree with the Crazyometer.

Aspect	Bonkers Jobs Score	Your Score
Are your friends impressed?	6 (Sounds like a good job)	
Do your parents dislike it?	5 (Yes, but they want me to earn money)	
Do you earn much money?	4 (Just about OK)	
Nice place to work?	5 (Indoors – that'll do)	
Job opportunities increasing?	5 (Staying the same)	
How brainy have you got to be?	6 (Need to train but no university)	
Crazyometer Total Score	31	

HEALTH AND SAFETY INSPECTOR

So what could possibly be disgusting about this job? After all, isn't it these people's jobs to stop **disgusting** things take place in the first place?

Well, sometimes names are designed to make us think one thing when in fact another is true. In the same way that **GREENLAND** is really full of snow and glaciers, so a health and safety inspector's job involves dealing with a lot of unhealthy and unsafe situations.

For example, every UK restaurant, takeaway and supermarket is rated out of five by the Food Standards Agency. If they score less than three they fail.

HOW MANY IN THE UK FAIL EACH YEAR?

a) 9%
b) 18%
c) 27%

Only 9% fail the test – so that's not too disgusting, but what if you visited one of those that failed? What would you find? The following are from real situations:

• The fridge contained fungi that had turned

green and infected the rest of the food.

- Cooking oil was covering the floor and mould was all over the walls.
- The restaurant was overrun with rats.

Fancy eating there? Well that's not all. If you're inspecting then the chances are you'll be out and about having a look around places to check they are safe, and if they are not then you may get hurt.

Even if you survive a visit you will have to record what you found, taking photographs of anything disgusting and recording sound levels that may be disturbing.

Mind you, they'll pay you reasonably for your troubles – starting from £25k, all the way up to a possible £70k a year.

AND THE JOB IS IMPORTANT. IT KEEPS THE WORKPLACE SAFE. DID YOU KNOW THAT LAST YEAR...

- 142 people were killed at work?
- 78,000 were injured?
- 1.2 million working people suffered from a work related illness?

If you fancy making a difference to the lives of workers then you'll need to study at university and be physically able to get out and about to visit places. As the world economy grows we'll need to feed people healthily and keep them safe at work, so these jobs will be around for some time yet.

But – and there is a **BIG** but – whilst the job does give you the opportunity to visit and record some disgusting places it also involves:

- Sitting in an office.
- Working out statistics.
- Writing reports.

NOW THAT SOUNDS REALLY DISGUSTING!

Bonkers Jobs Scorecard for Health and Safety Inspector

Now you've learnt about the job it's time to score it. Below we have worked out a Crazyometer score for the job – do you agree? Just mark each aspect of the job out of 10, 1 meaning 'rubbish' and 10 meaning 'brilliant'. Then total up your score to see if you agree with the Crazyometer.

Aspect	Bonkers Jobs Score	Your Score
Are your friends impressed?	3 (Sounds dull to them)	
Do your parents dislike it?	6 (They think it is sensible)	
Do you earn much money?	6 (Around / above average)	
Nice place to work?	6 (The office yes, but otherwise…)	
Job opportunities increasing?	5 (Steady)	
How brainy have you got to be?	6 (Need to go to university)	
Crazyometer Total Score	32	

ABATTOIR WORKER

Death, death and more death. Sounds worse than disgusting. What if you were the one bringing it, unleashing it and then tidying up after it? If that sounds appealing then abattoir worker is the role for you. But you may be wondering what an abattoir worker does, as the term abattoir is hardly commonly used.

Originally it's a word that comes from France and we use it to be polite: calling someone an abattoir worker sounds a lot more pleasant than slaughterhouse worker!

Slaughterhouse is what the word abattoir means. So if you are working there then your day job is to kill animals. Some may think that's disgusting, but it is not necessarily a bad thing... who doesn't enjoy a delicious Sunday roast. YUM, YUM!

It's worth pointing out that the abattoir worker does not randomly go round killing animals. In fact it's quite the opposite. There are all manner of government checks and rules that ensure that animals are killed humanely and safely.

WHICH ANIMAL DO WE SLAUGHTER THE MOST IN THE UK FOR FOOD?

a)   Cows/cattle.

b)   Pigs.
c)   Sheep/lambs.
d)   Birds/chickens.

It's birds – over 950 million of them! I bet you didn't know there were so many birds in the UK. And where are the next coming from? With numbers like that this job isn't going to go into decline anytime soon.

However, most chickens meet their fate in an automated poultry (another word of French origin – this time meaning birds) slaughter and processing factory. Those abattoir workers that cut animals throats, dissect the carcass and clean up after are working with over twenty-seven million pigs, cows and lambs a year!

Still interested? Then as long as you're physically fit, with a steady hand, you can start working Monday to Fridays 9 – 5pm and you'll be:

- Herding animals off lorries.
- Stunning and killing them using a bolt pistol.
- Splitting carcasses using an electric saw.
- Washing carcasses looking for disease.
- Cleaning floor areas, tools and equipment of blood.

When you get to the weekend you can put your feet up and spend the £20k you earn a year on a roast meal.

Bonkers Jobs Scorecard for Abattoir Worker

Now you've learnt about the job it's time to score it. Below we have worked out a Crazyometer score for the job – do you agree? Just mark each Aspect of the job out of 10, 1 meaning 'rubbish' and 10 meaning 'brilliant'. Then total up your score to see if you agree with the Crazyometer.

Aspect	Bonkers Jobs Score	Your Score
Are your friends impressed?	8 (The boys are)	
Do your parents dislike it?	5 (Reliable work)	
Do you earn much money?	5 (OK but won't become rich)	
Nice place to work?	3 (Er, no)	
Job opportunities increasing?	5 (As long as people don't become vegetarian)	
How brainy have you got to be?	3 (Need a steady brain to go with a steady hand)	
Crazyometer Total Score	29	

PORTABLE TOILET SERVICE DELIVERY DRIVER

Have you been to an outdoor event recently? A fair, a gig or maybe even a bonfire night display? **Did you need to spend a penny or do a number two?** If so, it's likely that you used a portable toilet.

And you wouldn't have been alone. How many portable loos do you think there are in the UK?

a)   1,000.
b)   10,000.
c)   100,000.

The answer is over 100,000 in use, now! And those 100,000 can come in different shapes and sizes, from blue box single loos to mobile toilet blocks, from beech panelling to wrap around mirrors. Despite this they all have one thing in common. **THEY NEED TO BE DELIVERED AND MAINTAINED.**

As delivery means loading, driving, unloading and balancing the toilet, experience in a construction/building site environment is a useful background for this job. As would some knowledge of plumbing, and an enquiring and investigative mind. After all, you might be called to find out what's wrong if they're not flushing correctly!

You will have to maintain and empty/pump out

the toilets. This is important as portable toilets keep their waste inside the bathroom. Failure to maintain them correctly can lead to a sewage smell in the toilet. Having a strong sense of smell is perhaps one quality it is best not to have when applying for this job!

Career wise, the demand for portable toilets has been on the increase. Invented in the 1950s and first used mainly in the construction industry, they're now used in increasingly diverse areas. With more outdoor events scheduled each year this could result in overtime work, taking your pay to over £25k a year with a 'wee' bonus. All in all the future looks bright for the industry – after all the human race is always going to need somewhere to go!

MOBILE TOILET FACTS:

- The first mobile toilet was made out of wood and metal. Unfortunately, these proved too absorbent – disgusting!
- Eurgh! You can purchase second-hand mobile toilets.

Bonkers Jobs Scorecard for Portable Toilet Service Delivery Driver

Now you've learnt about the job it's time to score it. Below we have worked out a Crazyometer score for the job – do you agree? Just mark each Aspect of the job out of 10, 1 meaning 'rubbish' and 10 meaning 'brilliant'. Then total up your score to see if you agree with the Crazyometer.

Aspect	Bonkers Jobs Score	Your Score
Are your friends impressed?	2 (No!)	
Do your parents dislike it?	5 (They see the need for it)	
Do you earn much money?	4 (Not enough for that job)	
Nice place to work?	3 (Only if you like the outdoors	
Job opportunities increasing?	6 (People always need them)	
How brainy have you got to be?	4 (Need hands-on skills)	
Crazyometer Total Score	24	

ARTIST

An artist, a disgusting job? Surely artist must belong in the 'nice jobs to have' chapter or the 'enhancing the world' chapter?

Well no. Not that artists themselves are disgusting – quite the opposite. They help us to see and understand the world.

Saying that, not many people liked Van Gough's work until after his death, and the term 'Impressionist' was used to mock the work of the great French artists Monet, Manet and Degas. Although in the end they quite liked the insult, so much so they adopted it to describe their art!

BUT MAKING ART CAN INVOLVE SOME DISGUSTING PROCESSES. WHAT DO YOU THINK ABOUT THESE?

- In the 1990s Damien Hirst was famous for pickling a cow and calf sliced in half. **That's disgusting!**
- In the Middle Ages, Michael Angelo and Leonardo Da Vinci would hand grind powdered pigments, mixing them with egg yolk, adding white wine or vinegar.
- In the 1990s the artist Herman Nitsch would

have people bathe in blood.

Still interested?
Then you need to get practicing those artistic skills.
What you produce – sculpture, video, painting, etc. – will determine which art school you can go on and study at.

While the world has always wanted and treasured artists, becoming an artist who can live off what they sell is difficult. Many artists do other jobs (e.g. teach) whilst producing art in their own time.

Some, however, do go on to become world famous and rich like David Hockney.

BORN IN BRADFORD ONE OF HIS PAINTINGS WAS SOLD FOR MORE THAN...

    a)   £1 million?
    b)   £2 million?
    c)   £5 million?

£5 million pounds – now that's not too disgusting is it!

Bonkers Jobs Scorecard for Artist

Now you've learnt about the job it's time to score it. Below we have worked out a Crazyometer score for the job – do you agree? Just mark each Aspect of the job out of 10, 1 meaning 'rubbish' and 10 meaning 'brilliant'. Then total up your score to see if you agree with the Crazyometer.

Aspect	Bonkers Jobs Score	Your Score
Are your friends impressed?	6 (Yes, they think it's not real work)	
Do your parents dislike it?	2 (No)	
Do you earn much money?	3 (Not unless you reach the top)	
Nice place to work?	5 (Could be anywhere)	
Job opportunities increasing?	6 (People always need them)	
How brainy have you got to be?	8 (Pretty smart to be the best)	
Crazyometer Total Score	30	

Choose Your Disgusting Job

Now you've ventured into the world of disgusting jobs it's time to think about which would be disgusting enough for you. To do that you need to complete the table below. Just take the scores you gave each disgusting job and place them in the table below.

Job	Magic Letter	Crazyometer score	Your score
Maggot Farmer	E	38	
Abattoir worker	R	29	
Health and Safety Inspector	C	32	
Beautician	S	31	
Portable Toilet Service Deliverer	I	24	
Artist	A	30	

Do you agree with our Crazyometer scoring? The good news is that the only right answer is your answer! We all see the world differently and it's your opinion that matters here.

So the disgusting job you have scored the highest is:

....

Look in the Crazyometer and you'll see there's a Magic Letter next to that job – what is it? You need to collect these magic letters. In the last chapter we will use these to help you find your own bonkers job.

Write your magic letter here:

....

Scary Jobs

When you hear of scary jobs you may think of jobs that cause the most fatalities (deaths) and injuries in the UK. You might be surprised to learn that the jobs with the highest death rates in the UK include the following:

- Builder.
- Farmer.
- Refuse (Bin) collector.
- Miner.
- Motor vehicle mechanic.

There are thousands of people who work in these industries though, so the fatalities and injuries suffered are actually very rare. So are you ready to read more about the jobs mentioned above?

No?

Good!

IT'S GOING TO BE SCARY!

STUNT PERSON

Let's start with a stunt person…

This is a man or a woman who replaces an actor during a dangerous or extremely athletic scene. Some actors actually enjoy doing their own stunts and then film crews don't need to get in a stunt person.

Q1: WHICH OF THE FOLLOWING THREE WELL KNOW ACTORS LIKE TO DO THEIR OWN STUNTS? ANSWER AT END.

a)   Jackie Chan (Lego Ninjago Movie, Karate Kid 2).

b)   Angelina Jolie (Maleficent 2, By the Sea).

c)   Tom Cruise (Mission Impossible, The Mummy).

WHAT A STUNT PERSON DOES INVOLVES:

- Fighting – martial arts or boxing.
  Falling – trampoline or high diving.
- Riding and driving – horse riding, driving cars or riding motorcycles.
- Agility and strength – gymnastics or rockclimbing.

- Water – swimming or sub-aqua.

Injuries are actually very common in this work and range from minor cuts and bruises, to broken bones, serious injuries and in some cases **DEATH.**

Did you know that Daniel Radcliffe's stunt double suffered a very serious injury in the filming of the final *Harry Potter* film?

Q2: WHICH INJURY DID HE SUFFER? ANSWER AT END.

    a)   Broken arm.
    b)   Paralysed.
    c)   Broken ribs.

A stunt person can't expect to have a regular 9 to 5 job. Most often they are approached by a film crew to undertake a particular scene.

This means that their earnings vary a lot, starting at around £20k a year, going right up to £60k a year for regular work. The job can be really glamorous and involve being flown to Hollywood – or a tropical island – to do a short scene! It could also involve being sent to the desert in blistering heat, or out in a snow storm in the Antarctic!

Often the director will insist that the scene is recorded many times before calling '**CUT**'.

Imagine what this must be like for a stunt person?! Falling off a cliff over and over again ... and again! OUCH!

ANSWERS:

Q1: The answer is in fact all three! Did you know that Jackie Chan actually started out as a stunt person before he became an actor?
Q2: The answer is unfortunately B: The stunt person could not walk after their injury.

Bonkers Jobs Scorecard for Stunt Person

Now you've learnt about the job it's time to score it. Below we have worked out a Crazyometer score for the job – do you agree? Just mark each Aspect of the job out of 10, 1 meaning 'rubbish' and 10 meaning 'brilliant'. Then total up your score to see if you agree with the Crazyometer.

Aspect	Bonkers Jobs Score	Your Score
Are your friends impressed?	8 (They think it is awesome)	
Do your parents dislike it?	8 (Parents would hate it)	
Do you earn much money?	7 (Good, when the work is there)	
Nice place to work?	7 (Film sets, mountains, fast cars, what's not to like?	
Job opportunities increasing?	3 (Lots of people want to be a stunt man)	
How brainy have you got to be?	3 (More crazy than brainy!)	
Crazyometer Total Score	36	

WASTE RECYCLING OFFICER

'Who'd want to be a waste recycling officer?' We hear you say. 'It's hardly an important job, is it?' Well, what a load of rubbish!

Q1: HOW MANY TONNES OF WASTE DO YOU THINK IS RECYCLED EACH YEAR FROM UK HOUSEHOLDS? ANSWER AT END.

a)   Over 30 million tonnes.

b)   Over 13 million tonnes.

c)   Over 3 million tonnes.

We need waste recycling officers to sort through everyone's rubbish. We know that recycling is a good thing and helps to save the planet, so shouldn't this be a superhero job, rather than a scary job?

NOPE!

OK, in recycling there are a lot of glass and sharp objects, so is that why it is scary? **No again.**

It's actually about how we get rid of stuff. Items around the house can be very harmful if they are not disposed of correctly.

HERE ARE A FEW EXAMPLES:

Batteries:

Yes, we need them for toys, remote controls and for gaming controls, but they do contain metals, such as mercury, that can be very harmful to eyes and skin, and they release gasses that are not good for the environment.

Fridge-freezers:

Who would have thought that the place we keep all our food is actually quite dangerous? Fridge-freezers contain chemicals to keep them cool. These chemicals are well-protected, but when a fridge stops working and is thrown away the chemicals need to be released safely.

Most of these metals, gasses and chemicals are not only very dangerous if they come into contact with your skins, eyes and mouth, but they can catch fire easily. A waste recycling officer needs to make sure that household goods are disposed of safely in order to avoid this.

The pay isn't great, especially considering how scary it can be. To start you can expect to earn around £19k a year, but if you manage a recycle centre you could earn up to £45k a year.

ANSWERS:

Q1 – A: Over 30 million tonnes.

Bonkers Jobs Scorecard for Waste Recycling Officer

Now you've learnt about the job it's time to score it. Below we have worked out a Crazyometer score for the job – do you agree? Just mark each Aspect of the job out of 10, 1 meaning 'rubbish' and 10 meaning 'brilliant'. Then total up your score to see if you agree with the Crazyometer.

Aspect	Bonkers Jobs Score	Your Score
Are your friends impressed?	5 (Boring!)	
Do your parents dislike it?	5 (Dangerous, but for a good cause)	
Do you earn much money?	4 (Is it worth the danger?)	
Nice place to work?	3 (Smelly and dirty, hmm!)	
Job opportunities increasing?	7 (Good chance I can get a job)	
How brainy have you got to be?	5 (Don't have to go to university)	
Crazyometer Total Score	29	

POLICE OFFICER

A police officer is one of the more normal jobs that features in Bonkers Jobs, but when you think about it, what they do is quite scary!

HOW MANY POLICE OFFICERS HAVE BEEN KILLED ON DUTY IN THE UK SINCE 1945? ANSWER AT END.

a)   Over 300.
b)   Over 3000.
c)   Over 30000.

To be a police officer you need to be good with people. You come into contact with them a lot!

Imagine all the **scary** things you could have to deal with as a police officer.

- Investigating crimes and offences.
- Making arrests and interviewing witnesses and suspects.
- Searching for missing people.
- Going out to accidents and fires.

Police work involves dealing with **criminals** – some carrying **weapons**. As a police officer it is very likely that you will see a dead body, attend a road accident or witness a fire at some point in your career. How on earth do they cope with the things they see?

But it's not all bad. Police officers do lots of COOl stuff – like drive fast cars, attend football matches and concerts, use handcuffs, but most of all… use a Taser! Tasers hurt people and should not be glamorised, but they can be effective.

QUESTION: ARE POLICE ALLOWED TO USE TASERS ON CHILDREN UNDER 18?

Answer: Yes! Why not talk to friends and discuss this. Should this be allowed?

True or False : **POLICE HAD TO TASER A FORTY-FIVE-YEAR-OLD MAN IN THE UK WHO WAS INVOLVED IN A**

FIGHT WITH A "STOP" ROAD SIGN?

This is actually true!

Police officers earn a starting wage of around £19k, rising to around £35k with more experience. They don't need any particular qualifications as such. Instead they have to pass entry tests based on a number of things like physical fitness, commonsense and how they react in certain scenarios.

There will always be a need for police officers, but criminals are most inconsiderate and often operate at night, meaning that the hours are very varied!

ANSWER:

A: Over 300 Police Officers killed since 1945.

Bonkers Jobs Scorecard for Police Officer

Now you've learnt about the job it's time to score it. Below we have worked out a Crazyometer score for the job – do you agree? Just mark each Aspect of the job out of 10, 1 meaning 'rubbish' and 10 meaning 'brilliant'. Then total up your score to see if you agree with the Crazyometer.

Aspect	Bonkers Jobs Score	Your Score
Are your friends impressed?	6 (If they are not impressed, arrest them)	
Do your parents dislike it?	5 (Long hours, so may not see much of you)	
Do you earn much money?	5 (Free Tazers too)	
Nice place to work?	4 (Could be sat in car all day)	
Job opportunities increasing?	5 (The country will always need police officers)	
How brainy have you got to be?	6 (More a combination of skill or personality)	
Crazyometer Total Score	31	

BOMB DISPOSAL EXPERT

HOW WOULD YOU LIKE TO BE A BOMB DISPOSAL EXPERT?

One false move and you're history! It really doesn't get much scarier than that!

Bomb disposal experts have to be incredibly patient. They need to analyse a situation very quickly, without panicking – doing the right thing and saving hundreds of lives.

...AND STAND WELL BACK...

Guy Fawkes is probably one of the most famous bomb-makers in our history, attempting to blow up the Houses of Parliament, but did you know that:

- Experts suggest the bomb would have not

exploded if it had been lit, as the gunpowder had decayed! There would have been no need for a bomb disposal expert for that job!

Most bomb disposal experts work in the armed forces and either in a warzone, or in public spaces to deal with unexplained objects that could be explosive.

Although this job is really scary it can also be quite cool. Most bomb disposal experts work with robots. After all it's probably preferable for a robot to be blown to pieces than a human being, don't you think?

Bomb disposal experts can also be involved in blowing things up. This might seem weird, but a **CONTROLLED EXPLOSION** is often something they are required to do – making sure that no one gets hurt.

As a bomb disposal expert you get to wear a special suit. Not the type your mum, dad or neighbour wears to the office, but body armour that protects you from explosive threats.

To become a bomb disposal expert we recommend you join the armed forces and get specialist training. Pay in the Armed Forces is about average, but bomb disposal officers are expected to get paid a bit more due to the dangers of the job. They earn around £30k - £40k a year for their work.

TRUE OR FALSE

- Bombs that were launched over one hundred years ago during World War I are still going off today?

The answer is true!

British and German forces launched more than a billion shells and bombs at each other as they fought during World War I. Some of these lie buried in farmland. In the Belgium town of Ypres 360 people have died from bomb related incidents since the end of the war. There is a special unit of bomb disposal experts in Ypres to help deal with this.

Bonkers Jobs Scorecard for Bomb Disposal Expert

Now you've learnt about the job it's time to score it. Below we have worked out a Crazyometer score for the job – do you agree? Just mark each Aspect of the job out of 10, 1 meaning 'rubbish' and 10 meaning 'brilliant'. Then total up your score to see if you agree with the Crazyometer.

Aspect	Bonkers Jobs Score	Your Score
Are your friends impressed?	8 (Pretty awesome)	
Do your parents dislike it?	3 (Best not tell your parents)	
Do you earn much money?	6 (Should be more, surely?)	
Nice place to work?	3 (Mostly in warzones)	
Job opportunities increasing?	5 (Has to be good thing)	
How brainy have you got to be?	7 (if you get it wrong...)	
Crazyometer Total Score	32	

COMEDIAN

Knock, knock. Who's there? It's a (scary) comedian. Not someone who likes to play pranks on people and scare them to death, but just trying to be funny can be really **SCARY!**

Everyone likes to think they are funny.

Some make people laugh, but how difficult must it be to stand up in front of thousands of people and tell jokes? **IT MUST BE ABSOLUTELY PETRIFYING!**

Now think about a comedian you like – Miranda? Mr Bean? Jim Carey? – what do they have in common?

Yes that's right, they're funny. And that's what you need to be, but comedians can be funny in different ways. Here's a list of different types of comedy, link up the word with its meaning. Answers at end.

PHYSICAL COMEDY : Saying jokes to an audience.
SATIRICAL COMEDY : TV series taking a funny look at groups of people.

STAND-UP COMEDY = Laughing at how processes/organisation works.
SITUATION COMEDY = Falls over in a funny way.

Most comedians do a few of the above.

Charlie Chaplin – heard of him? He was the most famous man in the world in the early twentieth century. Most of his films were 'silent' – no words used. He was a master of physical comedy, delivering funny walks, silly faces and hilarious falls. Chaplin though became more than just a comic.

WHICH OF THE BELOW DID HE ALSO ACHIEVE?

a)   Creating a movie studio?
b)   Creating the music that accompanied his films?
c)   Insulting Hitler?

Yes, all three! He created **UNITED ARTISTS** – a production company to make movies – won an Oscar for his music, and scripted, directed and starred in *The Great Dictator*, a film that took the micky out of Hitler. Hitler was so scared he had Chaplin banned from Germany!

How do you become a comedian? Well, you do need to be funny – either look funny, move funny or be quick witted enough to say funny things. Then work at whatever it is that makes you **funny**. And this is where the hard bit begins.

There is no set career path to become a comic. There isn't a set qualification to take that you can parade around saying, 'I have a qualification in comedy so you must laugh at me.' In fact many comedians have qualifications and training in other things.

DID YOU KNOW THAT:

- Rowan Atkinson has a degree in electrical engineering?
- Harry Hill is a qualified doctor?
- Miranda Hart has a degree in political science?
- Keith Lemon was once voted business man of the year for his invention of an anti-theft car device?

Many comedians start to work for **FREE**. Isn't that a joke, they give up their own time for nothing. They go along to comedy clubs, pubs where they can try out their jokes. And if they are funny then they'll get invited back and get paid. Starting pay for comedians is around £10k - £20k, but famous comedians' earn far more than that – some get millions!

Oh and if you don't make it then it's back to the day job – *scary!*

ANSWERS:

PHYSICAL COMEDY = Falls over in a funny way.
STAND-UP COMEDY = Saying jokes to an audience.
SATIRICAL COMEDY = Laughing at how processes/organisation works.
SITUATION COMEDY = TV series taking a funny look at groups of people.

Bonkers Jobs Scorecard for Comedian

Now you've learnt about the job it's time to score it. Below we have worked out a Crazyometer score for the job – do you agree? Just mark each Aspect of the job out of 10, 1 meaning 'rubbish' and 10 meaning 'brilliant'. Then total up your score to see if you agree with the Crazyometer.

Aspect	Bonkers Jobs Score	Your Score
Are your friends impressed?	9 (If you are good)	
Do your parents dislike it?	5 (They might tell you to get a proper job)	
Do you earn much money?	6 (Good, if you are funny)	
Nice place to work?	6 (OK, unless you get things thrown at you)	
Job opportunities increasing?	6 (Has a comedian even won Britain's Got Talent?)	
How brainy have you got to be?	7 (Always have to think up new material)	
Crazyometer Total Score	39	

PRIME MINISTER

The final scary career to explore is arguably the most important job in the country... the prime minister! OK, as the prime minister, it is not likely that you will be doing many daredevil stunts, or at risk of falling from high buildings or anything, but if you think about it, it really is one of the most terrifying jobs of all!

HOW MANY PRIME MINISTERS HAVE THERE BEEN IN THE UK WITHIN THE LAST 100 YEARS? ANSWER AT END.

a)   25.
b)   42.
c)   102.

The prime minister is responsible for all the policies and decisions made by the government. The government make lots of decisions every day for the country, from how hospitals and doctors' surgeries are run, to what we should be studying in the classroom at school. The prime minister also has the final decision on whether to use the atomic bomb!

Imagine if they got that decision wrong. SCARY STUFF!

Have you ever tried to make a decision for you and your friends? Imagine you had to decide what you and four of your friends are going to do for a day. Where you are going to go, for how long, what you will eat, etc. The chances are that at least one of your friends will disagree with some of the things you decided and might be unhappy with you. So what would it be like to make decisions for the whole country? That is over sixty-five million people! Pretty scary, eh?

SO HOW DO YOU GET TO BE A PRIME MINISTER?

Well, there isn't a particular course you need to learn or qualification you need to get, but generally you need to be intelligent, good at talking in public and not afraid to be **UNPOPULAR!** It is actually very difficult to become a prime minister. The good news is that you get paid very well. It is estimated that the prime minister is paid around £150,000 every year! Imagine what you could do with that money.

Although it would be very scary to be a prime minister, it could also be totally awesome! Imagine what new policies you could bring in to make the country more fun?

HOW ABOUT SOME OF THESE:

- Monday to Friday is the weekend and that Saturday and Sunday is for school and work!
- Parents by law are not allowed to ask children to tidy their room.
- All theme parks and cinemas must be open all year round and are not allowed to charge people to get in.

WHAT NEW POLICIES WOULD YOU BRING IN? WRITE THEM DOWN HERE.

ANSWER:
A- 25.

Bonkers Jobs Scorecard for Prime Minister

Now you've learnt about the job it's time to score it. Below we have worked out a Crazyometer score for the job – do you agree? Just mark each Aspect of the job out of 10, 1 meaning 'rubbish' and 10 meaning 'brilliant'. Then total up your score to see if you agree with the Crazyometer.

Aspect	Bonkers Jobs Score	Your Score
Are your friends impressed?	7 (You might be popular)	
Do your parents dislike it?	3 (Oh no, parents pleased too)	
Do you earn much money?	9 (That would be nice)	
Nice place to work?	8 (Even get a house – number 10)	
Job opportunities increasing?	1 (Only 25 prime ministers in 100 years)	
How brainy have you got to be?	9 (Need to be clever, calm and collected)	
Crazyometer Total Score	37	

Choose Your Scary Job

Now you've ventured into the world of scary jobs it's time to think about which would be frightening enough for you. To do that you need to complete the table below. Just take the scores you gave each scary job and place them in the table below.

Job	Magic Letter	Crazyometer score	Your score
Stunt Person	R	36	
Waste Recycling Officer	C	29	
Police Officer	S	31	
Bomb Disposal Officer	I	32	
Comedian	A	24	
Prime Minister	E	37	

Do you agree with the Crazyometer scoring? The good news is that the only right answer is your answer! We all see the world differently and it's your opinion that matters here.

So the scary job you have scored the highest is:

....

There is a Magic Letter next to that job – what is it?
You need to collect these magic letters. In the last
chapter we will use these to help you find your own
bonkers job.

Write your magic letter here:

....

Cool Jobs

Do you want to impress your friends? Do you like being the first in the class to have the latest gadget? Hope to be the trend setter? If so you may want a **cool** job.

Cool jobs come in all shapes and sizes – some involve you looking **cool**, some you doing **cool** things and others have you in the **coolest** of places.

Some jobs sound **cool** but when you find out more the shine comes off.

DID YOU KNOW THAT?

- Lumberjack was once found to be the worst job in America due to low pay, high danger and few job opportunities.
- Research suggests that the happiest workers in the UK are vicars and priests.

So, which job will match your **cool** career ideas?

FASHION DESIGNER

If you really want to be a trend setter then what better way than designing clothes everyone in the **IN CROWD** will want to wear? When people think you know what is **hip**, they'll wear whatever you tell them to. And we mean whatever:

DID YOU KNOW?

- That British designers have made a dress out of chocolate?
- That Lady Gaga wore a dress made of meat?
- That some clothes are made out of recycled material – that means newspaper, bottle caps and broken china pieces?

Of course not everyone wants to design clothes for celebrities to wear. Most fashion designers create clothes to be sold in the high street, online shops and supermarkets. There are a lot of people out there needing clothes to wear, so there are a lot of clothes to be sold. How many? Let's think pants and bras.

HOW MANY PANTS AND BRAS WERE SOLD IN THE UK LAST YEAR?

- 1 million.
- 10 million .
- 100 million.

It's over 100 million, and, yes, someone sat down and designed those pants and bras – it could be you!

SO TO BECOME A FASHION DESIGNER DO YOU NEED?

a)   Lots of experience or qualifications in design.

b)   Crazy ideas about what people might wear.

c)   Be good at cutting out and sticking.

ANSWER:

A, B and C. Many fashion designers go onto

university or do a lot of on the job training so that they know every style and technique in depth. You need to be creative as your ideas have to stand out from everyone else's and, of course, you not only need to have the idea for a piece of clothing, but also be able to make it yourself, in order to show what it really looks like.

As everyone needs clothes, fashion design is a truly global industry. Every year the fashion industry puts on shows in some of the coolest places: from Paris to New York, Milan to London. Models wear the designer's clothes so the designers can become well known.

CAN YOU MATCH THESE FAMOUS NAMES WITH THE FASHION THEY INVENTED? ANSWERS AT END.

Mary Quant	The Bikini
Levi Strauss	Mini Skirt
Lois Reard	Blue Jeans

With the world population increasing there will be no let-up in the demand for new fashion designs. But not everyone will go global with their fashion designs.

Most work for High Street names and earn around £35k a year. However if you change the way we dress you'll be earning millions.

ANSWERS:

Mary Quant – Mini Skirt.
Levi Strauss – Blue Jeans.
Lois Reard – The Bikini.

Bonkers Jobs Scorecard for Fashion Designer

Now you've learnt about the job it's time to score it. Below we have worked out a Crazyometer score for the job – do you agree? Just mark each Aspect of the job out of 10, 1 meaning 'rubbish' and 10 meaning 'brilliant'. Then total up your score to see if you agree with the Crazyometer.

Aspect	Bonkers Jobs Score	Your Score
Are your friends impressed?	8 (Yes, they like your designs)	
Do your parents dislike it?	2 (No, they also like your designs)	
Do you earn much money?	6 (A decent wage – with lots of money if you get famous)	
Nice place to work?	7 (Indoors)	
Job opportunities increasing?	5 (Population is increasing. Everyone needs clothes!)	
How brainy have you got to be?	7 (need to be creative and practical)	
Crazyometer Total Score	35	

MOBILE ICE CREAM SELLER

If it's hot outside there's only one way to cool down. And that's with an **ice cream.**

DID YOU KNOW THAT WE SPEND OVER £1 BILLION ON THE STUFF EACH YEAR!

How would you like to travel around in the sunshine, meeting people and giving them what they want?

Sounds appealing? Why not become a mobile ice cream seller?

OK, you might need some product knowledge.

CAN YOU ANSWER THE FOLLOWING QUESTIONS? ANSWERS AT END.

- a) Ice cream originated in which country in the 1600s?
- b) The world's most popular ice cream topping is…?
- c) How many licks does it take to finish a single scoop?

OH, AND WHAT'S THE DIFFERENCE BETWEEN SOFT ICE CREAM, HARD ICE CREAM AND A SORBET?

Once you know the product, it's time to get out there and sell it – either by cycling around on your specially made trike or using an ice cream van. Of course, there is a price difference. If you want to buy a trike it's about £3,000, while a brand new van costs roughly £60,000.

Once you get the transport then you are away.

No formal qualifications are required, though you are running your own business, so you will need to manage your money and make sure you meet any hygiene requirements. Also, remember you'll be meeting the public, so excellent selling skills is a must.

One downside is that there are fewer ice cream sellers than there used to be. In the 1950s there were about 20,000 ice cream van operators in Britain. Now there are less than 5000. Also people are more likely to stock up their freezers with ice creams, and with modern restrictions on where you are allowed sell things aren't as easy as they were.

On the plus side, the mobile ice cream market still accounts for over £100 million of sales per year. And, of course, you can still choose the chime you want your van to play, usually from thirty-two different chimes such as the *Teddy Bears Picnic* or *Greensleeves*. How cool is that?!

Oh, and did you know that in the 1980s there were ice cream wars in Glasgow? Rival gangs were using the vans to sell more than tubs, iced lollies and cones. They were also selling drugs and stolen goods.

ANSWERS:

a)   Italy.
b)   Chocolate syrup.
c)   50.

Soft ice cream has a different texture to hard ice cream as it is lower in milk fat and has more air in it. Sorbet is a frozen dessert made from sweetened water with flavouring.

Bonkers Jobs Scorecard for Mobile Ice Cream Seller

Now you've learnt about the job it's time to score it. Below we have worked out a Crazyometer score for the job – do you agree? Just mark each Aspect of the job out of 10, 1 meaning 'rubbish' and 10 meaning 'brilliant'. Then total up your score to see if you agree with the Crazyometer.

Aspect	Bonkers Jobs Score	Your Score
Are your friends impressed?	8 (Who doesn't want a cheap ice lolly?)	
Do your parents dislike it?	5 (They also want cheap ice cream)	
Do you earn much money?	4 (Not as much as they used to)	
Nice place to work?	8 (Cool – and driving around meeting people)	
Job opportunities increasing?	2 (Not good)	
How brainy have you got to be?	4 (Need to be able to do basic maths and English)	
Crazyometer Total Score	31	

GAME DESIGNER

- What industry is worth over $100 billion?
- Which industry affects popular culture in the way pop music did in the 1960s?
- Which industry allows you to appear in movies, shoot people and manage a Premier League football team?

THE COMPUTER GAME INDUSTRY OF COURSE!

An industry that dominates our lives like nothing else. We spend hours playing games each day, testing ourselves, trying again and again to get the high score.

BUT WHO THINKS THEM UP? WHERE DO THESE IDEAS COME FROM?

Think it through. There's a lot to do:

- What's the vision?
- What's the content and rules of a game?
- What's the storyline?
- What will the artwork be like?
- What script is needed?

Blimey, no wonder those games cost so much money

– there's so much to do! Actually far too much for one person!

Game creators start with a vision and story. From there they work with teams to bring that vision to life.

WHICH OF THE FOLLOWING JOBS ARE IN THAT TEAM?

- Artist.
- Designer.
- Animator.
- Composer.
- Sound effects technician.
- Programmer.
- Project Manager.
- Marketing officer.

ANSWER:
ALL OF THEM!

The UK video game industry is the third largest in the world and has had great success in sales of hardware and software. However, game designers come from all over the globe.

The guy who invented Space Invaders in 1978 was Tomohiro Nishikado from Japan.

WHAT DO YOU THINK HE STUDIED TO MAKE THIS HAPPEN?

a)   Computing.
b)   Engineering.
c)   Media Studies.

THE ANSWER IS ENGINEERING.

To work in game design you don't necessarily need knowledge of computers, but maths is vital. The application of maths is central to writing any game program. Even though the product appears cool, the process involves the practical use of mathematical formula. And maths is a universal language – it means the same in French as it does in Chinese, so whatever you create can go around the world.

How cool is that?

Game designer is definitely a job in demand, with 30,000 people employed in games-related jobs in the UK. Wage levels vary, but you could be looking at well over £50k if you work on a successful game. And I mean well over – the creator of Minecraft bought himself a mansion worth $70 million!

How many logins per month does Minecraft have?

a)   2 million.
b)   20 million.
c)   200 million.

ANSWER: OVER 200 MILLION
COOL!

Bonkers Jobs Scorecard for Games Designer

Now you've learnt about the job it's time to score it. Below we have worked out a Crazyometer score for the job – do you agree? Just mark each Aspect of the job out of 10. 1 meaning 'rubbish' and 10 meaning 'brilliant'. Then total up your score to see if you agree with the Crazyometer.

Aspect	Bonkers Jobs Score	Your Score
Are your friends impressed?	10 (Yes, they like a geek)	
Do your parents dislike it?	1 (No, they like the job opportunities)	
Do you earn much money?	8 (Yes please)	
Nice place to work?	8 (It's a growing business)	
Job opportunities increasing?	2 (Not good)	
How brainy have you got to be?	8 (Smart with maths and creative with it too)	
Crazyometer Total Score	37	

ANTARCTIC RESEARCHER

Well, this one might not be cool in the same way as others, but Antarctic researcher certainly ranks as one of the **COLDEST** jobs in the world.

The Antarctic has the lowest naturally occurring temperature ever recorded on the surface on Earth: -89.2 °C (-128.6 °F). So, if you want the coldest job, there is only one place to go.

You may be thinking that it's too cold to work in Antarctica, but no. A number of governments maintain permanent research stations there. Many of the stations are staffed around the year.

SO, HOW MANY PEOPLE ARE WORKING THERE?

   a)   24,000.
   b)   4,000.
   c)   40,000.

This varies from approximately 4,000 during the summer season to 1,000 during winter.

If the cold is your thing, how can you get to shiver eighty-nine degrees below?

The best way is to learn your sciences at school. Antarctic stations exist purely for scientific research. Geologists study rocks, marine biologists

swot up on the creatures living in the frozen seas, and Environmental Scientists work out what is happening to the climate.

But even if you are not a scientist you may still find work out there. For instance, support workers outnumber those doing the research. Chefs, doctors, mechanics and heating engineers are all needed to keep the operation going.

So, what's it like to live out there? Well, the British Antarctic Survey operates six research stations. One of them – Halley – is located on a floating ice shelf and has hydraulic legs that can be raised to overcome snow accumulation. Oh, it also has a snow runway!

As the climate changes and resources become scarce, countries are showing greater interest in the Antarctic. Some believe that there's a vast supply of gas and oil there. Environmentalists, however, are opposed to such development there.

Pay rates are similar to the scientists within the UK, although while you're in the Antarctic, you don't have much to spend your money on, so you may find yourself coming home with most of it.

Cool!

Bonkers Jobs Scorecard for Antarctic Researcher

Now you've learnt about the job it's time to score it. Below we have worked out a Crazyometer score for the job – do you agree? Just mark each Aspect of the job out of 10, 1 meaning 'rubbish' and 10 meaning 'brilliant'. Then total up your score to see if you agree with the Crazyometer.

Aspect	Bonkers Jobs Score	Your Score
Are your friends impressed?	8 (Sounds 'cool' to them)	
Do your parents dislike it?	4 (No, but they don't like me being far away)	
Do you earn much money?	7 (Yes, and nothing to spend it on, so a great way to save)	
Nice place to work?	5 (If you like making snowmen)	
Job opportunities increasing?	7 (Yes)	
How brainy have you got to be?	8 (Depends on the job, but some need to go to university)	
Crazyometer Total Score	39	

ENTREPRENEUR

Entrepreneurs start their own businesses, offering innovative products and services. They drive the economy forward, making money for us all. How cool is that?

Often entrepreneurs go to university but this is not always the case. Some study product design. Others make things in their garage. There is no set path to become an entrepreneur, but there are personal qualities that you will need.

These are:

- **Communication** – you need others to understand your plans and products.
- **Sales** – to earn a living you'll need to convince people to buy the products and services your business offers.
- **Risk** – setting up a new business and developing a project is a step into the unknown, are you willing to take that risk?

Entrepreneurs really are key to wealth creation in a country. They create 40% of the new jobs in the global economy. And they work in all areas. Try matching these well-known entrepreneurs with the work they do: Answers at end.

RICHARD BRANSON = Vacuum cleaners/heaters.

JAMES DYSON = Travel/media.

ALAN SUGAR = Retail/sports equipment.

MIKE ASHLEY = Technology/property.

While starting your own business can result in you becoming a billionaire it is worth noting that most small companies go bust in the first year.

However, small companies are so important to the economy that governments are always looking to help people who want to start up.

SO FANCY BECOMING ONE? Well, try our entrepreneur quiz to see if you'd make a great entrepreneur.

RANK EACH OF THE TEN FOLLOWING QUESTIONS ON A SCALE OF 1-5

1 = I love it. 5 = I hate it.

Circle your answer for each question. When you have answered all ten questions add up your scores to find out if you're a natural entrepreneur.

1. DO YOU LIKE TAKING RISKS?

1   2   3   4   5

2. DO YOU LIKE TAKING RESPONSIBILITY?

1   2   3   4   5

3. DO YOU LIKE WORKING ON YOUR OWN?

1   2   3   4   5

4. DO YOU LIKE TAKING THE INITIATIVE?

1   2   3   4   5

5. DO YOU LIKE RISING TO A CHALLENGE?

1   2   3   4   5

6. DO YOU LIKE WORKING HARD?

1   2   3   4   5

7. DO YOU LIKE GETTING REWARDS FOR YOUR EFFORTS?

1   2   3   4   5

8. DO YOU LIKE FINDING THINGS OUT?

1   2   3   4   5

9. DO YOU LIKE PAPERWORK?

1   2   3   4   5

10. DO YOU LIKE MEETING DEADLINES?

1   2   3   4   5

Your Total Is

_____

Scored 20 or under: You are well-equipped to run your own business.

Scored 20-35: You will love some aspects of running your own business but hate others

Scored 35+: You will need a lot of help to run your

own business.

Did you know?

Former US president George Bush once said, 'The problem with the French is that they don't have a word for entrepreneur'. The problem is the word entrepreneur comes from French!

ANSWERS :

RICHARD BRANSON = Travel/media.

JAMES DYSON = Vacuum cleaners/heaters.

ALAN SUGAR = Technology/property.

MIKE ASHLEY = Retail/sports equipment.

Bonkers Jobs Scorecard for Entrepreneur

Now you've learnt about the job it's time to score it. Below we have worked out a Crazyometer score for the job – do you agree? Just mark each Aspect of the job out of 10, 1 meaning 'rubbish' and 10 meaning 'brilliant'. Then total up your score to see if you agree with the Crazyometer.

Aspect	Bonkers Jobs Score	Your Score
Are your friends impressed?	8 (Yes, they like the money I earn)	
Do your parents dislike it?	4 (No, but they know it can be risky)	
Do you earn much money?	7 (Potential is good)	
Nice place to work?	7 (Yep, going where I want to)	
Job opportunities increasing?	7 (Always needed)	
How brainy have you got to be?	5 (Need to be clever, but don't have to go to university)	
Crazyometer Total Score	38	

ACCOUNTANT

Accountant! Really? How is an accountant a bonkers job, never mind a COOl job?

Well, we all know that most accountants work by themselves, working out sums and writing reports. But what makes this job so COOl isn't the day to day operations, but what they can do with those numbers.

For example:
Did you know it was the work of an accountant that got the fearsome gangster Al Capone put in gaol ('gaol' is the original English spelling of the word 'jail', which is the American version)? He found out that he hadn't been paying his taxes.

Forensic accountants work across the UK, making sure that everybody pays their tax properly.

Did you know?
It was these forensic accountants who found that the former champion jockey Lester Piggott had kept £3 million that he owed the government – and promptly sent him to gaol.

FANCY A BIT OF THIS ACTION? You'll need to get a good grade at GCSE maths, a University degree, or train up as an accounting technician.

Now, getting to the top takes many years of training, but the rewards could be worth it. Top accountants are paid in excess of £100k, and everyday accountants will be earning in advance of £30k. COOl!

Why do you think they are so well paid? It's simple really. **THEY KNOW ABOUT MONEY!** How to save you money, and how to make your money turn into more money. Now that's knowledge worth paying for!

Sadly, with all this money going around, some accountants turn bad. They become corrupt and decide to make the money work for their own gain. This results in some big scandals, try this for size:

Enron was an American company. Its accountants made its accounts deliberately hard to understand so everyone thought the company was doing well. By the time people realised what the accountants had done over $74 billion had been lost!

Accountants can also surprise us in other ways.

Did you know:

An accountant invented bubblegum in 1924 and the comedian Eddie Izzard once studied accountancy?

Given all you've read, you'll probably not be surprised to learn that accountancy and financial jobs are in demand. In fact over the past twenty years it has been one of the UKs biggest growing sectors.

Bonkers Jobs Scorecard for Accountant

Now you've learnt about the job it's time to score it. Below we have worked out a Crazyometer score for the job – do you agree? Just mark each Aspect of the job out of 10, 1 meaning 'rubbish' and 10 meaning 'brilliant'. Then total up your score to see if you agree with the Crazyometer.

Aspect	Bonkers Jobs Score	Your Score
Are your friends impressed?	5 (Nah)	
Do your parents dislike it?	3 (Yes, safe job in their eyes)	
Do you earn much money?	7 (Can do)	
Nice place to work?	6 (Yep — indoors)	
Job opportunities increasing?	5 (Staying the same)	
How brainy have you got to be?	6 (Need to be OK with maths but don't have to go to university)	
Crazyometer Total Score	32	

Choose Your Cool Job

Now you've ventured into the world of cool jobs it's time to think about which would be cool enough for you. To do that you need to complete the table below. Just take the scores you gave each cool job and place them in the table below.

Job	Magic Letter	Crazyometer score	Your score
Fashion Designer	A	35	
Ice Cream Van Driver	S	31	
Game Designer	R	42	
Antarctic Researcher	I	39	
Entrepreneur	E	38	
Accountant	C	32	

Do you agree with the Crazyometer scoring? The good news is that the only right answer is your answer! We all see the world differently and it's your opinion that matters here.

So the cool job you have scored the highest is:

....

There is a Magic Letter next to that job – what is it? You need to collect these magic letters. In the last chapter we will use these to help you find your own bonkers job.

Write your magic letter here:

....

Delicious Jobs

Delicious jobs. Sound tasty, don't they? Although this being *The Bonkers Book of Jobs*, we don't just mean careers where you might eat something.

No, we're talking about that delicious task you've always wanted. You know, like throwing a custard pie in someone's face.

We could bore you with facts about delicious jobs, such as:

- A professional beer taster can get paid over £30,000 a year.
- More than a billion Mars bars are sold a year.
- Two billion people worldwide routinely eat insects.

But we'd rather tell you about a tasty task that involves creating alien species! Have a look at our delicious jobs and decide which is mouth-watering enough for you.

DOG FOOD TASTER

Be careful to read the small print on any job advert. If it says food taster it might be worthwhile checking out exactly what food you will be asked to taste. After all there are a lot of pets to be fed in the UK.

HOW MANY CATS AND DOGS LIVE IN THE UK?

a) 12 million.
b) 16 million.
c) 20 million.

The answer is b, 16 million – that's a lot of pets to feed (so many that the pet food market in the UK is worth nearly £3 billion). Not only that, this figure's rising all the time! In the last ten years sales of dog treats have doubled, with dry cat food increasing by 80%.

DO DOG FOOD TASTERS REALLY EAT THE FOOD?

Yes – with a knife and fork and off a plate. But wait – aren't the tasters taking a risk? Actually quite the opposite; there is legislation governing the manufacturing of pet food, with dog food specifically having to be passed as fit for human consumption.

It is not just taste they are checking for. They also check the **FLAVOUR**, texture and **consistency**. They go through quite a lot, so there's no need to swallow and most dog food tasters spit out the samples after washing them around their mouths.

Fancy it?

Well, most dog food tasters are university educated and have a background in the food industry. They don't spend their whole time tasting. They report their findings and work with a team to improve the recipe, while thinking up new ones.

As a dog food taster you start on around £20k, but if you really shine at the job you could earn over £50k. Now that's delicious.

What is not so delicious is that in some countries people still eat dogs.

HOW MANY DO YOU THINK ARE EATEN BY PEOPLE ACROSS THE GLOBE EACH YEAR?

a)   10 million.
b)   25 million.
c)   50 million.

The answer is 25 million – crazy!

Bonkers Jobs Scorecard for Dog Food Taster

Now you've learnt about the job it's time to score it. Below we have worked out a Crazyometer score for the job – do you agree? Just mark each Aspect of the job out of 10, 1 meaning 'rubbish' and 10 meaning 'brilliant'. Then total up your score to see if you agree with the Crazyometer.

Aspect	Bonkers Jobs Score	Your Score
Are your friends impressed?	4 (Some think I'm mad)	
Do your parents dislike it?	5 (Er, they see the need for it)	
Do you earn much money?	7 (Yes, that's OK)	
Nice place to work?	6 (Yep, indoors)	
Job opportunities increasing?	5 (Only if the number of dogs die)	
How brainy have you got to be?	6 (Clever enough to want to eat food)	
Crazyometer Total Score	33	

CAKE DECORATOR

WOW, this does sound delicious! Sumptuous cakes decorated to the highest of standards, and all of them very different.

Maternity cakes, gun cakes, computer cakes, purse cakes, storytelling cakes, camera cakes, Yoda cakes – to name but a few.

Cake decorators could probably bake a cake into any shape you want. Why not draw one yourself below.

Cake decorators need a great imagination, a good eye for detail and a steady hand. Many are self-employed, but some work in kitchens or for supermarket chains, earning from £15k to £25k a year. A crazy job, not too crazy a wage, but don't despair.

If you need more **DOSH** you could also get into pastry and make the craziest dish to come out of any kitchen – the custard pie!

Custard pie jokes date back to the circus era. These days they're more likely to feature in a film, or when a celebrity gets pranked. This is called 'Pieing'. Which of these famous names has had a custard pie put in their face?

BILL GATES, FOUNDER OF MICROSOFT.
RUBERT MURDOCH, OWNER OF NEWSPAPERS AND SKY.
ANDY WARHOL, FAMOUS ARTIST.

Actually it is all of them. Who would you like to pie? Draw what they would look like with a pie in their face below.

Like for cake decorators, on the job experience is vital to being a pastry chef and, as you work, you'll need to gain qualifications. The job demand is steady, and you're likely to find full-time work in a kitchen/restaurant earning around £20k a year. In a posh restaurant you could earn a lot more.

Oh, and you won't just be making custard pies. Pastry chefs often get a chance to research and develop new recipes. In large restaurants they may also be in charge of the dessert menu, including cheese boards and the dessert wine. Delicious!

Did you know that there's a world custard pie throwing championship? It takes place each year in the village of Coxheath, Kent. Crazy!

Bonkers Jobs Scorecard for Cake Decorator

Now you've learnt about the job it's time to score it. Below we have worked out a Crazyometer score for the job – do you agree? Just mark each Aspect of the job out of 10, 1 meaning 'rubbish' and 10 meaning 'brilliant'. Then total up your score to see if you agree with the Crazyometer.

Aspect	Bonkers Jobs Score	Your Score
Are your friends impressed?	5 (They like cake)	
Do your parents dislike it?	5 (They also like cake)	
Do you earn much money?	5 (Not too much)	
Nice place to work?	4 (If you enjoy getting messy)	
Job opportunities increasing?	5 (Give the people cake!)	
How brainy have you got to be?	4 (Good with your hands and ideas)	
Crazyometer Total Score	28	

GENETIC ENGINEER

Genetic engineer? Motor vehicle engineer, civil engineer, electrical engineer YES, but a genetic engineer?

WHAT DO THEY DO?

Well, they change a plant or animal's genes to make them different, or even use the genes to create an entirely new species. Yes, that's right, a new species!

So what are these genes? They are in every living creature, plant or animal. They are too small for you to see them. They determine everything about you when you are born, from what you look like to the colour of your eyes and even the size of your feet.

It sounds quite radical but humans have been playing about with plant and animal genes for hundreds of years. But since the 1970s we've been speeding this process up.

In fact the applications of this engineering are now widespread.

DID YOU KNOW?

- Genetically modified pigs are being

bred with the aim of increasing the success of pig-to-human organ transplantation.

- Some bacteria have been genetically changed to create black and white photographs.

- Genetic engineering has been used to make fish glow.

Genetic engineers are also interested in the food we eat. How can they make plants grow quicker, produce more crops and resist insects? How can they make delicious food?

While the idea of sweeter fruit and tastier peas sounds good, some people are concerned that engineering these changes could affect the environment. Will crops react differently? Will animals and insect numbers be reduced? So, for this reason, only a few trials of these new crops, take place in the UK each year.

However, it is an area of possible job growth. Each year thirty million tonnes of genetically engineered animal feed is imported into Europe (including the UK) and as the science develops so will the desire of those who want to try the new crops.

FANCY IT?

Well you'll need to study your sciences at school. And at university take a science degree, perhaps in genetics. Then after that maybe study genetics even more – they do like you to know what you are doing in this job. At the end of it you'll have some cash though, starting from £50k and going through to over £100k.

There are two sides to food. One is the agricultural (growing crops), the other is pastoral (raising animals). Genetic engineers have already cloned animals.

Which animals do you think? Sheep, pig, rat, wolf, horse? Yes, all of them plus eighteen other animals! None of these clones are being farmed at present, but who knows? Maybe one day all cows will look exactly the same. Crazy!

Bonkers Jobs Scorecard for Genetic Engineer

Now you've learnt about the job it's time to score it. Below we have worked out a Crazyometer score for the job – do you agree? Just mark each Aspect of the job out of 10, 1 meaning 'rubbish' and 10 meaning 'brilliant'. Then total up your score to see if you agree with the Crazyometer.

Aspect	Bonkers Jobs Score	Your Score
Are your friends impressed?	9 (Oh, yes)	
Do your parents dislike it?	4 (No)	
Do you earn much money?	9 (Yes, I'm in demand)	
Nice place to work?	6 (Yes, not cold or hot)	
Job opportunities increasing?	7 (Yes)	
How brainy have you got to be?	9 (Very smart, lots of studying needed)	
Crazyometer Total Score	44	

RESTAURANT OWNER

Running your own restaurant. Sounds a steady job, doesn't it? You employ someone to cook and someone to serve food. Delicious!

But when you start a restaurant up you have over 25% chance of it going bust. That means a quarter of new restaurant owners have gone bust within a year. That's starting to sound a little crazy.

Also:

- What if your restaurant fails a health and safety check?
- What if your kitchen puts out food that poisons someone?

You don't know? Then you'd better find out quickly because as the owner you are responsible.

It gets better. Big restaurant chains employ restaurant managers, but as yours is probably a small restaurant, you won't have the money, so you'll be covering this task. That means working evenings, weekends and public holidays – including Christmas and Easter!

That's the crazy part over with. More delicious

is the fact that you'll pick up around £40k a year. Also, the number of people eating out in restaurants has increased over the last thirty years, so it looks likely that there'll be increasing opportunities in the future.

Being a restaurant owner means you are part of the hospitality economy, and that is worth £46 billion to the UK. It also directly employs 2.5 million people, so you should have no problem finding staff.

What will make your restaurant a great success? All of the factors below are required. Rank them 1: most important, to 5: the least important. Answers at end.

LOCATION
SEATING
SIGNAGE
MENU
SERVICE

Now your restaurant is a success you can think about expanding, or setting up a restaurant chain like Burger King or Pizza Hut. What would your restaurant chain be called? **MAYBE WRITE IT BELOW.**

Ours is going to be Deliciously Bonkers about Food!

LOCATION – People have to get there!

SIGNAGE – People have to be able to see the exact building you are in.

SEATING – People like to have space when eating and they also need to be comfortable.

MENU – If the food is no good they won't come back.

SERVICE – If the food is late or the waiters are rude they won't be back.

Bonkers Jobs Scorecard for Restaurant Owner

Now you've learnt about the job it's time to score it. Below we have worked out a Crazyometer score for the job – do you agree? Just mark each Aspect of the job out of 10, 1 meaning 'rubbish' and 10 meaning 'brilliant'. Then total up your score to see if you agree with the Crazyometer.

Aspect	Bonkers Jobs Score	Your Score
Are your friends impressed?	7 (They like a good meal)	
Do your parents dislike it?	4 (They also like a good meal)	
Do you earn much money?	6 (If the people are coming in, I'm doing alright)	
Nice place to work?	6 (Yes, although hours can be awkward)	
Job opportunities increasing?	8 (People eating out is increasing)	
How brainy have you got to be?	5 (Need to get on with people and know your Maths and English)	
Crazyometer Total Score	36	

CHEESE MAKER

HOW MANY CHEESES DOES THE UK MAKE? 700.
HOW MANY CHEESES DOES FRANCE MAKE? 1000.
HOW MANY CHEESES DOES THE WHOLE OF EUROPE MAKE? Over 3000.

That's a lot of cheese, and we in Europe eat more cheese that anywhere else. In weight it works out at 37.6 pounds per person a year. That's the same weight as a two-year-old child!

SO, WHY NOT BECOME A CHEESE MAKER?

Making cheese is a global practice, invented by the Egyptians and spread throughout the world. And it's not just cow's milk that you make cheese from. You can also make cheese from goats, sheep or even buffalo milk.

Cheese making may date back over five thousand years, but since 1815 – when the Swiss established the first cheese factory – cheese has been made industrially. Most cheese makers in the UK work in a food manufacturing team. They are skilled technicians who make sure that there is a constant supply of raw material, with computer-aided machines producing cheese at optimum speeds.

You need to get to grips with these machines, but once you've completed your higher level training, you'll mostly work weekdays and earn over £20k a year. As the process of making cheese is scientific, knowledge of the sciences will come in handy. As a global industry you could take your skillset and travel the world making cheese – how crazy is that?

Although most cheese production is done on a large scale, in recent years there has been a rise in the production of more local cheeses. It's not that hard a process.

CAN YOU PUT EACH STAGE IN THE CORRECT ORDER? ANSWER AT END.

Drain it.
Add bacteria.
Ferment it.
Heat milk.
Salt it.

You can then choose what cheese you want to make. Will it be as crumbly as Wenleysdale, as mouldy as Stilton or as smelly as Epoisses (a cheese so smelly that France has banned it from all its public transport)? Whatever cheese you make, make sure it's delicious!

Did you know that a cheese is banned in the EU? CasuMarzu was traditionally made in Sicily and it is filled with live maggots – delicious!

ANSWER:
Heat milk, add bacteria, drain it, salt it, ferment it.

Bonkers Jobs Scorecard for Cheese Maker

Now you've learnt about the job it's time to score it. Below we have worked out a Crazyometer score for the job – do you agree? Just mark each Aspect of the job out of 10, 1 meaning 'rubbish' and 10 meaning 'brilliant'. Then total up your score to see if you agree with the Crazyometer.

Aspect	Bonkers Jobs Score	Your Score
Are your friends impressed?	5 (Some like cheese, some don't)	
Do your parents dislike it?	3 (No, they think it's a productive job)	
Do you earn much money?	6 (Yep, not bad)	
Nice place to work?	5 (Can be smelly)	
Job opportunities increasing?	6 (Yep, people always like cheese)	
How brainy have you got to be?	5 (Average will be fine)	
Crazyometer Total Score	30	

DIETICIAN

Eating food can be a delicious activity. However, eat too much of the wrong food and you could damage your body and mind. If you only eat junk food you will:

- Put on weight.

- Increase your chance of getting diabetes.

- Be more likely to have mental health problems.

Of course, junk food is OK as long as it's just one part of a balanced diet. In fact we like junk food so much that, on average, each family in the UK spends almost £1500 on it each year. That's a lot of chips, burgers and chicken nuggets!

BUT HOW DO WE KNOW THAT EATING JUNK FOOD WILL DO US HARM? WHO HAS THE FACTS ABOUT THIS?

It's a dietician, of course.

Dieticians work mainly for the National Health Service. They present the facts so you can eat more healthily. This is important as many allergies and diseases can be controlled by people eating the correct food for them.

Not all dieticians work for the hospitals though. They can be found in diverse areas: at NASA, in sports teams and even on the big screen.

well, it IS made of green cheese···

Why NASA? Well, it's not possible to cook in space, so dieticians work out the correct balance of freeze dried food needed to ensure the astronauts stay healthy. They collect and analyse data about their food intake and levels of exercise, and design a menu for them. What would be on your space flight menu?

What about sport? Clearly what we eat affects our bodies and to be lean and mean we need to make sure we eat the right food. In addition athletes need to make sure they are eating enough food. Exercising all day means they need to re-fuel. Did you know an Olympic athlete needs to consume 12,000 calories a day? The average person needs just 2,500 calories. That means they need to eat over four times more than most people. **WHEN DO THEY FIND TIME TO TRAIN WHEN EATING THAT MUCH?**

Why cinema? Well, actors need to look like the characters they are playing. So if the character is fatter or thinner then they'll have to change their weight – and do so in a healthy way that doesn't harm their bodies. Dieticians advise them on which foods they should eat to help them do this. The actor Robert De Niro put on over four stone during the filming of one movie – crazy!

Dieticians are good at sciences at school and study further at university. They earn between £22k and £40k a year. With the healthcare sector growing, and people increasingly understanding the value of eating the right foods, the demand for dieticians is rising.

Bonkers Jobs Scorecard for Dietician

Now you've learnt about the job it's time to score it. Below we have worked out a Crazyometer score for the job – do you agree? Just mark each Aspect of the job out of 10, 1 meaning 'rubbish' and 10 meaning 'brilliant'. Then total up your score to see if you agree with the Crazyometer.

Aspect	Bonkers Jobs Score	Your Score
Are your friends impressed?	6 (Yep, they like to look their best)	
Do your parents dislike it?	3 (Yep – a steady job)	
Do you earn much money?	6 (Above average)	
Nice place to work?	7 (Yep – inside)	
Job opportunities increasing?	6 (The work is becoming important)	
How brainy have you got to be?	6 (Need to study to get the knowledge)	
Crazyometer Total Score	34	

Choose Your Delicious Job

Now you've ventured into the world of delicious jobs it's time to think about which would be delicious enough for you. To do that you need to complete the table below. Just take the scores you gave each delicious job and place them in the table below.

Job	Magic Letter	Crazyometer score	Your score
Dog Food Taster	C	33	
Cake Decorator	A	27	
Genetic Engineer	I	43	
Restaurant Owner	E	33	
Cheese Maker	R	30	
Dietician	S	34	

Do you agree with the Crazyometer scoring? The good news is that the only right answer is your answer! We all see the world differently and it's your opinion that matters here.

The delicious job you have scored the highest is:

....

There is a Magic Letter next to that job – what is it? You need to collect these magic letters. In the last chapter we will use these to help you find your own bonkers job.

Write your magic letter here:

....

WeiRD Jobs

Just imagine if you had a job that other people didn't know even existed. Their jaw would hit the floor as soon as you told them your occupation!

SEE IF YOU CAN LINK THESE WEIRD JOB TITLES TO THE SENTENCES BELOW. ANSWERS AT END.

Teddy Bear Technician.
Gumologist.
Waterslide Tester.
Odor Tester.

a.   **** travels the world visiting many theme and holiday parks. You will need your swimming gear as you may be testing safety of the rides.

b.   As an **** you will need a good sense of smell and a strong stomach as this job can be disgusting!   You will test the performance of products like deodorants and see which ones work and which ones don't.

c. This next job requires an eye for detail and good needlework skills. As a **** you will be helping young children to get their best friends back to good health!

d. **** experiment with different chemicals and ingredients to create new flavours for chewing gum.

As weird as these jobs are, they are nothing compared to these **WEIRD** and whacky workers in this chapter.

TAKE A LOOK FOR YOURSELF AND SEE WHAT YOU THINK.

ANSWERS:
- a) Waterslide Tester.
- b) Odor Tester.
- c) Teddy Bear Technician.
- d) Gumologist.

MASCOT

Whether it is for your favourite team or at a holiday park, many people are actually employed as **MASCOTS**. They range from bears, birds or elephants. Do you remember the mascots from the Olympic Games? When you were watching your favourite athletes, such as Mo Farar and Usain Bolt earning their living, did you also think about those earning a living as a mascot?

WHICH OF THE FOLLOWING USA MASCOT FACTS ARE TRUE?

a) Every school and college has their own mascot.

b) There is a school to train mascots of the future.

c) There has been a mascot wedding.

ANSWER: THEY ARE ALL TRUE!

Mmm, there can't be many easier jobs in the world than a mascot! You get paid for wearing a silly costume, running around doing stupid things and waving to everyone. But although the job may seem cool, imagine how hot it would be in some of those costumes. You wouldn't want to be wearing a costume all day in the middle of a hot summer.

TRUE OR FALSE?

Mascots from sporting teams and big companies meet up every year for the Mascot Grand National. The answer is true!

How amazing is that? Can you imagine up to one hundred mascots, ranging from giant pizzas to ridiculous characters, all racing and jumping over obstacles to compete for the highest honour in the mascot world?

Although there probably isn't a massive demand for mascots in the UK, a mascot would surely get a job at somewhere like Disneyland! They must have hundreds of mascots working for them every day. Imagine all the mascot friends you would make? It can't be bad!

I wonder if mascots take their costumes home. Imagine a mascot travelling to and from work in their car, or even better on the bus or train. They would get some strange looks!

Let's face it you would probably struggle making enough money as a full-time career mascot, and the hours might be quite tricky too, mainly during holidays and at the weekends. If you were employed full-time as a mascot you would earn around £13k - £15k a year. Other than the mascot school in the USA, there really isn't much in the way of training to be a mascot. Despite all this it would still be worth it to be able to compete in the Mascot Grand National!

Bonkers Jobs Scorecard for Mascot

Now you've learnt about the job it's time to score it. Below we have worked out a Crazyometer score for the job – do you agree? Just mark each Aspect of the job out of 10, 1 meaning 'rubbish' and 10 meaning 'brilliant'. Then total up your score to see if you agree with the Crazyometer.

Aspect	Bonkers Jobs Score	Your Score
Are your friends impressed?	8 (Hilarious)	
Do your parents dislike it?	5 (Get a real job!)	
Do you earn much money?	2 (Unhappy mascot)	
Nice place to work?	7 (Free entry!)	
Job opportunities increasing?	5 (Not really)	
How brainy have you got to be?	6 (Do you really need to be smart to wave?!)	
Crazyometer Total Score	33	

FACE FEELER

Ever seen TV ads for razors, shaving foams and moisturisers claiming to give you the best shave ever?

HOW ABOUT BEAUTY PRODUCTS SUCH AS CREAMS AND MOISTURISERS THAT CLAIM TO MAKE YOU LOOK TEN YEARS YOUNGER?

In order to make such claims you need face feelers to analyse people's faces. Imagine having to get that close to someone's face just to check how smooth it is?

Mind you it could be worse!

Imagine being the poor guy whose face has to try out the new razors! Equally as scary is being the person who tests the razors. Each year there are loads of people who sign up to trial skin care products.

Sure, you'll get paid, and you'll receive free skincare products. But imagine if you had an allergic reaction or the product was faulty. You could end up coming out in spots, or even worse the product could burn your skin.

Have you ever heard the expression 'in your face'? Well, that is what a face feeler has to do all day long!

Imagine if the person's face you were feeling had eaten garlic for lunch! How horrible would it be to get that close to someone with smelly breath? Or imagine if the person's face had a huge ZIT or SPOT, how embarrassing would that be?

TRUE OR FALSE:
Junk food causes acne?
False!

According to a leading New York dermatologist (someone who knows all about skin) no studies have shown a direct link between junk food and breakouts of acne. **SO HOW WOULD YOU BECOME A FACE FEELER?**

As crazy as it sounds, you would most likely need to have a good understanding of the human body and chemicals that cause a reaction to the skin. And you would need to do a lot of studying before you could start face feeing!

As a qualified face feeler the good news is that you could expect to get paid quite a lot of money, with starting salaries of around £25k a year, rising to £45k for more experienced workers. Let's face it (see what I did there) there are always new skincare products to test, so the chances of getting a job as a face feeler are quite good!

Bonkers Jobs Scorecard for Face Feeler

Now you've learnt about the job it's time to score it. Below we have worked out a Crazyometer score for the job – do you agree? Just mark each Aspect of the job out of 10, 1 meaning 'rubbish' and 10 meaning 'brilliant'. Then total up your score to see if you agree with the Crazyometer.

Aspect	Bonkers Jobs Score	Your Score
Are your friends impressed?	6 (Did I hear you right?!)	
Do your parents dislike it?	5 (Are you sure that it's a job?)	
Do you earn much money?	6 (Feeling face pays OK!)	
Nice place to work?	5 (Now wash your hands!)	
Job opportunities increasing?	6 (More face feelers!)	
How brainy have you got to be?	7 (Need to study at university)	
Crazyometer Total Score	35	

DICE INSPECTOR

You can't be serious! Someone has made this job up, right?

Wrong!

Very wrong in fact, as it is a huge industry.

Dice are not only used in everyday board games like Monopoly and Mouse Trap, but they are also used in casinos in the gambling industry.

DID YOU KNOW:

- A dice could earn you thousands of pounds?

- A dice could send you to prison?

Ever seen or heard of the film *Ocean's Eleven*? Or *Ocean's Twelve* or *Thirteen* for that matter?! These films are about a gang of criminals hitting Las Vegas by robbing the casinos for millions of dollars. In the films George Clooney and Brad Pitt blow up safes and con people to get their hands on the casino money.

Well, Brad and George, I have news for you. You could have done it far easier with one weapon – **a dice!**

YES, THAT IS RIGHT!

A dice is made extremely carefully so that each

side has the same weight and size. And when you roll it you always get a random number between 1 and 6, but some bright spark thought that if he/she changed the weight it might make it more likely to land on the number 6 each time.

The perfect crime, hey?

No!

I'm afraid the authorities caught on to this and now every casino has dice inspectors who examine each dice to make sure they are all as they should be. In fact, as well as the casinos employing dice inspectors, the gambling authorities also employ their own staff to check that the casino dice inspectors are doing their job right.

WHO WOULD HAVE THOUGHT THERE WOULD BE SUCH A DEMAND FOR THIS JOB?!

It does sound like a seriously sad job – going round casinos with your magnifying glass and weighing scales to check each dice, but think about it...

You get to travel quite a bit and not just anywhere, but glamorous hotspots like Las Vegas, Atlantic City or New York. We do also have dice inspectors in this country too, but the thought of travelling to Skegness and Blackpool doesn't sound quite as good though!

To do a job such as this you need to be extremely reliable and honest, and you need to have a good eye for detail. Taking all this into consideration, the role of a dice inspector is relatively official and therefore the money is quite good, with average earning of around £25k - £35K a year.

HERE'S AN INTERESTING FACT ABOUT DICE

Did you know that on a proper dice if you add each opposite side together it should always add up to the number 7? For example, the number 6 should be opposite number 1, 3 should be opposite 4, etc. Have a look at your dice at home and see if you have proper dice. Also test your family's knowledge; I bet no one knows this fact, so you can properly show off!

Bonkers Jobs Scorecard for Dice Inspector

Now you've learnt about the job it's time to score it. Below we have worked out a Crazyometer score for the job – do you agree? Just mark each Aspect of the job out of 10, 1 meaning 'rubbish' and 10 meaning 'brilliant'. Then total up your score to see if you agree with the Crazyometer.

Aspect	Bonkers Jobs Score	Your Score
Are your friends impressed?	8 (Quite cool)	
Do your parents dislike it?	7 (Important job)	
Do you earn much money?	7 (Quite well paid)	
Nice place to work?	7 (Don't gamble your money away)	
Job opportunities increasing?	5 (Not bad)	
How brainy have you got to be?	7 (Need to understand the science of dice)	
Crazyometer Total Score	41	

LEGO SCULPTOR

Yes, people are actually employed to build Lego! Lego has turned into a massive industry over the years, so much so that we have seen a Lego movie with Hollywood stars playing the roles!

HOW MANY LEGO BRICKS DO YOU THINK ARE PRODUCED EACH YEAR? ANSWER AT END.

a)   4.5 million.
b)   45 million.
c)   45 billion.

There is a Legoland in Windsor in the UK. It's a massive park filled with, yes, you guessed it... Lego! It has rides and activities that make it one of the UK's most popular theme parks.

At Legoland there are miniature sculptures of many famous places and things, all made from Lego! There are mini buildings like the Tower of London, Big Ben, the Eiffel Tower and The Empire State Building. All of these sculptures are made up of thousands and thousands of individual pieces of Lego.

To be a Lego sculptor you need to be very good with your hands as Lego building is incredibly fiddly. You also need to be very patient, as things can go wrong. Lego can break and you can waste hours of work.

If you happen to live near Legoland and are really, really good at building Lego, then you would have a reasonably good chance of getting a job as a Lego sculptor. **WHAT IF YOU LIVED MILES AWAY THOUGH?** Well, it might be a little more difficult, but there are lots of Lego stores all over the country, and they all need models built.

Of course, it would be awesome to work as a Lego sculptor, but it's not easy either. You need to have a powerful imagination! In return you will earn between £20k and £30K a year, not bad if you would do it for fun anyway!

ANSWER:

C. In 2012 45.7 billion bricks were produced! That works out as 5.2 million an hour. That is a serious amount of Lego!

Bonkers Jobs Scorecard for Lego Sculptor

Now you've learnt about the job it's time to score it. Below we have worked out a Crazyometer score for the job – do you agree? Just mark each Aspect of the job out of 10, 1 meaning 'rubbish' and 10 meaning 'brilliant'. Then total up your score to see if you agree with the Crazyometer.

Aspect	Bonkers Jobs Score	Your Score
Are your friends impressed?	8 (Awesome!)	
Do your parents dislike it?	6 (All that Lego they bought you paid off)	
Do you earn much money?	6 (More money to spend on Lego!)	
Nice place to work?	8 (Especially if you work at Legoland)	
Job opportunities increasing?	6 (They're building up nicely!)	
How brainy have you got to be?	6 (Perhaps more patient and skilled, than brainy)	
Crazyometer Total Score	40	

GOLF BALL DIVER

This job really does take **weirdness** to a whole new level!

HAVE YOU EVER PLAYED GOLF BEFORE? OR WATCHED IT ON THE TV?

It really isn't the most interesting sport in the world. Despite this, it is a multi-billion pound industry! Did you know that a basic pack of golf ball costs in the region of £10? The most expensive golf ball is over two hundred years old.

Q1. WHAT WAS IT SOLD AT AUCTION FOR:

    a)   £2,000.
    b)   £12,000.
    c)   £24,000.

On golf courses there are obstacles to make the game more difficult. The more obstacles there are, the more accurate you need to be to avoid them. The obstacles tend to be either big sand pits called 'bunkers', or ponds or lakes.

If a ball lands in a bunker the golfer can jump into the sand pit and take their shot from inside. This is really difficult. But if a golfer's ball lands in the pond or lake they receive a penalty point and have to use a new ball.

Just imagine how much better the game would be if when a ball landed in the water the golfer had to dive in, find their ball and try and take their shot knee-deep in the water!

But as entertaining as this would be, there would no longer be any need for golf ball divers! The balls that golf ball divers find are sold on as 'lake balls', which are cheaper as they are second-hand.

As strange as it may seem, the number of golf balls lost each day is quite staggering. In the UK one clever person decided to make a business out of selling on lake balls. This businessperson employs seven divers, who dive into golf course lakes up and down the country and are paid a small sum for every ball they find.

Q2. HOW MUCH MONEY DO YOU THINK THE BUSINESS MADE IN A YEAR? ANSWER AT END.

a)   £7,000.
b)   £70,000.
c)   £700,000.

All a golf ball diver needs is diving equipment and something to put all the balls in! You don't need to be super intelligent to do this kind or work either. All you need is to learn how to dive properly with an oxygen tank on your back, which is actually more difficult than it sounds! One big **NEGATIVE** though is that golf is an all year round sport. Imagine having to dive into a lake in the middle of winter to collect golf balls!

Q1 ANSWER:
Believe it or not it was in fact C – £24,000!

Q2 ANSWER:
C – £700,000!

Bonkers Jobs Scorecard for Golf Ball Diver

Now you've learnt about the job it's time to score it. Below we have worked out a Crazyometer score for the job – do you agree? Just mark each Aspect of the job out of 10, 1 meaning 'rubbish' and 10 meaning 'brilliant'. Then total up your score to see if you agree with the Crazyometer.

Aspect	Bonkers Jobs Score	Your Score
Are your friends impressed?	8 (How strange!)	
Do your parents dislike it?	6 (OK, if they like golf)	
Do you earn much money?	6 (Could be serious money)	
Nice place to work?	5 (No thank you, especially in winter)	
Job opportunities increasing?	5 (Not really)	
How brainy have you got to be?	4 (No university degree required here)	
Crazyometer Total Score	34	

DOG YOGA INSTRUCTOR

There cannot be such a job. **Are you barking mad?** Well maybe, but there *are* yoga instructors that specialise in teaching dogs.

SO WHAT EXACTLY IS YOGA?

Yoga is an old discipline from India. It uses breathing techniques, exercise and meditation and claims to improve health and happiness and reduce stress.

OK, I get that bit, so what has it got to do with dogs? I mean just how stressed do dogs actually get? Let's face it, they have a pretty easy life. They get their food brought to them, receive lots of attention, and never have to do anything tougher than chase after a stick, chase their tails and sniff other dog's poo!

Dog yoga was first introduced in America, but it is now also available in this country. According to instructors, dog yoga or **DOGA** is less about the breathing techniques and well-being of dogs and more about improving the bond between dogs and dog owners.

HOW MANY DOGS ARE THERE IN THE UK?

a)   0.9 Million.
b)   9 Million.
c)   9 Billion .

ANSWER:
B – 9 Million.

Just imagine what a dog yoga class is like. It would be chaos: dogs running around chasing each other, barking as loud as they can. What about the smell too? As cute and adorable as dogs are, they do have a certain aroma which must be quite **disgusting** when you have groups of them together! Also yoga classes tend to last around an hour. There must be a reasonable chance that at least one dog may need to go to the toilet in that time!

This could be a perfect job for dog lovers that like

exercise and meditation, but the hours would most likely be evenings and weekends. If you could get a reasonable-sized **DOGA** class and could do it often, there is potential to make a living. You would need to become a qualified yoga instructor of course, which you may be able to study at college or do a diploma online.

Imagine if you could convince every dog owner in the UK to do **DOGA**. You would be a very busy instructor! In reality it is not likely that many dog owners will take part in **DOGA**, so opportunities for work in this area are likely to be rare. If you could find enough customers to make it a full-time job you might expect to earn around £15k a year. Perhaps you can branch out to other animals? Cat yoga – **COGA**; or fish yoga – **FOGA**?

Bonkers Jobs Scorecard for Dog Yoga Instructor

Now you've learnt about the job it's time to score it. Below we have worked out a Crazyometer score for the job – do you agree? Just mark each Aspect of the job out of 10, 1 meaning 'rubbish' and 10 meaning 'brilliant'. Then total up your score to see if you agree with the Crazyometer.

Aspect	Bonkers Jobs Score	Your Score
Are your friends impressed?	6 (Barking mad!)	
Do your parents dislike it?	6 (Not to be sniffed at)	
Do you earn much money?	3 (Grrr!)	
Nice place to work?	4 (All that dog poo!)	
Job opportunities increasing?	3 (Struggle to upgrade the dog house!)	
How brainy have you got to be?	4 (Time to goof around!)	
Crazyometer Total Score	26	

Choose Your Weird Job

Now you've ventured into the world of weird jobs it's time to think about which would be weird enough for you. To do that you need to complete the table below. Just take the scores you gave each disgusting job and place them in the table below.

Job	Magic Letter	Crazyometer score	Your score
Mascot	A	29	
Face Feeler	I	35	
Dice Inspector	C	41	
Lego Scupltor	R	40	
Golf Ball Diver	E	34	
Dog Yoga Instructor	S	26	

Do you agree with the Crazyometer scoring? The good news is that the only right answer is your answer! We all see the world differently and it's your opinion that matters here.

So the weird job you have scored the highest is:

....

There is a Magic Letter next to that job – what is it? You need to collect these magic letters. In the last chapter we will use these to help you find your own bonkers job.

Write your magic letter here:

....

Stupid Jobs

There seem to be more and more stupid jobs advertised every day, but just what is a stupid job and how do you get one?

Well, first of all let us clear up that a stupid job is not something a stupid person does! We all know people who just do **daft** things all the time, but they'll probably end up with quite normal jobs. A stupid job is a job title that sounds very glamorous and important, but it is actually something very usual, but we just know it as something different. For example, can you guess what this stupid job is more commonly known as?

OPTICAL ILLUMINATOR ENHANCER

Well let's take each word in turn and try and figure it out:

OPTICAL – as in opticians, where you go to test your eyesight or vision.
ILLUMINATOR – to illuminate is to brighten up or shine.

ENHANCER – is something that improves or makes something better.

SO WE HAVE A VISION BRIGHTENING IMPROVER? WHAT ON EARTH IS THAT? CAN YOU GUESS?

It is, in fact, a window cleaner!

How utterly stupid is that? Why on earth don't they just call it a window cleaner? Well, some stupid people think that if they give a job a posh title they will make it sound more attractive and more people will apply to do it. Let's have a look at some more stupid jobs.

EDUCATION CENTRE NOURISHMENT CONSULTANT

This sounds to be a very important job and in many ways it is. Have you ever met an education centre nourishment consultant? The answer is most definitely **yes!**

IN FACT:

- They work in large places like schools, colleges and universities.

- They tend to wear a hat and an apron.

- You probably see or talk to one most days.

Yes, an education centre nourishment consultant is actually a dinner lady/man!

What a ridiculous job title for what is actually a very important job. The word **nourishment** pretty much means food that is necessary for growth, health and other good stuff. School dinners are much more than just sausage and chips, or pizza and chips, because **nourishment** helps children lead healthy lifestyles, which can also help children learn better at school.

A dinner lady/man has to think about all the

ingredients to make healthy meals for children. They also need to figure out how to buy all the ingredients and make sure that the dinners can be sold at a reasonable price.

Just imagine how difficult that would be? What would it be like if you were the education centre nourishment consultant for the largest school in the UK?

HOW MANY PEOPLE DO YOU THINK GO TO THE LARGEST SCHOOL IN THE UK?

    a)   1,500.
    b)   3,500.
    c)   7,500.

The largest school in the country is, in fact, in Nottingham in the East Midlands of England and has over 3,500 students, around two hundred teachers and approximately 100 admin staff and assistants. That is getting close to 4,000 people. Just think if they all wanted a school dinner how big the queue would be!

For anyone wanting to be an education centre nourishment consultant, the good news is that there are plenty of opportunities.

HOW MANY SCHOOLS DO YOU THINK THERE ARE IN ENGLAND ALONE?

    a)   £2,400
    b)   14,000
    c)   24,000

There is thought to be more than 24,000 schools in total in England. The hours you can expect to work are roughly 9am to 5pm and the money you get depends on if you in charge of the food for the whole school/college – £20 k - £35K a year – or if you are an assistant – £13 - 1 7k a year. You need to have a catering qualification, as well as being calm, creative and good with maths and science.

Bonkers Jobs Scorecard for Education Centre Nourishment Consultant

Now you've learnt about the job it's time to score it. Below we have worked out a Crazyometer score for the job – do you agree? Just mark each Aspect of the job out of 10, 1 meaning 'rubbish' and 10 meaning 'brilliant'. Then total up your score to see if you agree with the Crazyometer.

Aspect	Bonkers Jobs Score	Your Score
Are your friends impressed?	4 (You do what?!)	
Do your parents dislike it?	4 (Could have tried harder)	
Do you earn much money?	5 (OK, but can be short hours)	
Nice place to work?	4 (Lots of hungry children)	
Job opportunities increasing?	6 (Maybe the dinner queues will be shorter in the future!)	
How brainy have you got to be?	6 (The person who plans the meals has a lot to think about)	
Crazyometer Total Score	29	

BARISTA

A barista is a **stupid** job for lots of different reasons. Let's have a look in a bit more detail. OK, I know what you are thinking: a barista can't be a **stupid** job because they help people who are accused of a crime. **WRONG!** Yes, helping people in a court of law is not a stupid job. In fact you have to be very intelligent to do the job, but that is a **BARRISTER** not a barista!

Now we have cleared that up, what is the difference between a barrister and a barista?

Well, the answer is quite a lot. Despite the jobs sounding very similar, they are completely different and are not related in anyway, which is one of the reasons why a barista is a **stupid** job!

A barista is someone who works in a coffee shop serving drinks and snacks. The name 'barista' is the Italian word for a bartender. So why do we use the job title barista instead of something like coffee shop assistant or even bartender?

Ah, I get it. Is it because coffee comes from Italy? **No!**

Most of the world's coffee actually comes from South America, from countries like Brazil or Columbia, though Africa and Asia are also big exporters of coffee. Italy, however, is famous for coffee drinking. In fact it is Italy we have to thank for all those different types of coffee – like cappuccino, Americano and latte that confuses the British public every day.

Coffee is a massive business and is the second most exported substance in the world, with the first being oil. It is quite obvious why oil is the most important, but coffee second? That is just stupid! It doesn't even taste that good!

How much do you think one of the most expensive types of coffee is per cup?

a)   £5.
b)   £25.
c)   £50.

ANSWER:
C

This expensive coffee is known as 'Kopi Luwak'. Experts say that this coffee is the greatest because it includes part-digested coffee cherries eaten and digested by the Asian palm civet, which is a type of cat.

SO WHAT DOES THAT MEAN IN ENGLISH?

Well it means that coffee is a type of fruit and this type of cat is known to only eat the best type of coffee. So they wait until the cat needs a poo and use this to sell the most expensive type of coffee.

Yes you read that right – the best coffee in the world is basically cat poo! Utterly stupid!

There are thousands of coffee shops in the UK, with big coffee shop chains like Starbucks, Costa and Café Nero in most towns and cities. That means that the chances of becoming a barista are quite high, and you don't need many qualifications to get a job. What's most important that you are good with the public. The pay sadly isn't that great though, with salaries of around £13 - £15K a year, and the hours can be quite long.

Bonkers Jobs Scorecard for Barista

Now you've learnt about the job it's time to score it. Below we have worked out a Crazyometer score for the job – do you agree? Just mark each Aspect of the job out of 10, 1 meaning 'rubbish' and 10 meaning 'brilliant'. Then total up your score to see if you agree with the Crazyometer.

Aspect	Bonkers Jobs Score	Your Score
Are your friends impressed?	8 (Free hot chocolate!)	
Do your parents dislike it?	6 (Could have tried harder, but cheap coffee!)	
Do you earn much money?	4 (Not so good)	
Nice place to work?	8 (Long hours, but think of the tea breaks)	
Job opportunities increasing?	8 (There is always a new coffee shop appearing somewhere!)	
How brainy have you got to be?	4 (Not very)	
Crazyometer Total Score	38	

COLOUR DISTRIBUTION TECHNICIAN

This particular stupid job is a bit easier for you to guess. After all working with colour is a bit of a giveaway! **SO WHAT IS IT?**

Yes, it is actually a painter and decorator! This is a person that works with mainly paint, wallpaper and tools to make buildings look cleaner, more modern and give them a layer of protection. They work in people's houses, as well as shops, offices and factories.

Painters and decorators do not always work indoors though. For example the Forth Bridge in Scotland is over 2.5 kilometres long (about 1.5 - 2 miles) and it needs painting regularly to protect it.

HOW LONG DO YOU THINK IT TAKES THEM TO PAINT THE FORTH BRIDGE?

a) A week?
b) A month?
c) A year?

Trick question! None of the above. They have actually only recently stopped painting the bridge, despite the fact that it was built in 1890! This is because as soon as they have painted the bridge from one end to the other, it was time to start again!

Only in 2011 did they finish painting the bridge with extra strong modern paint that will last for over twenty years! That really is a **stupid** job!

You need to have a great deal of patience to be a painter and decorator. Think about it – before you even open a tin of paint you need to cover up carpets and furniture so you don't splash paint everywhere. Then there are all those **fiddly** things like light switches and sockets that get in the way.

HOW MANY DIFFERENT COLOURS DO YOU THINK ONE OF THE TOP BRANDS OF PAINT IN THE UK HAS IN THEIR RANGE?

a)   500.
b)   4,000.

c)   10,000.

B

Most learn on the job by watching other experienced painters and decorators. We know they need to have skills and patience, but do they really need such a **posh** job title?

Most of the time colour distribution technicians work inside. At least they won't freeze in the winter or get soaked in a thunder storm. Buildings will always need painting to protect them or to improve their appearance. The pay is quite low though, with a starting wage of around £15k, rising to £25k with experience.

Bonkers Jobs Scorecard for Colour Distribution Technician

Now you've learnt about the job it's time to score it. Below we have worked out a Crazyometer score for the job – do you agree? Just mark each Aspect of the job out of 10, 1 meaning 'rubbish' and 10 meaning 'brilliant'. Then total up your score to see if you agree with the Crazyometer.

Aspect	Bonkers Jobs Score	Your Score
Are your friends impressed?	6 (Let's go paintballing)	
Do your parents dislike it?	4 (Parents will want you to paint the house for free)	
Do you earn much money?	4 (Not great)	
Nice place to work?	6 (OK when working indoors)	
Job opportunities increasing?	5 (About the same)	
How brainy have you got to be?	4 (Don't drip paint on the floor)	
Crazyometer Total Score	29	

MEDIA DISTRIBUTION OFFICER

If we break down this job we can soon figure out what it is normally called. So here goes:

MEDIA:
Things like TV, radio, newspapers or the Internet. Basically anywhere we get information from.

DISTRIBUTION:
Pretty much means sharing things out in big numbers.

So put these together and what do you get? Yes, that's right. It is a paper boy/girl or someone that delivers leaflets! The chances are that you may have a paper round or know someone else that does. If you do have a paper round, the next time someone asks you if you have a part-time job, tell them that you are in fact a media distribution officer! I wonder what response you would get!

Q1. HOW MANY HOURS CAN YOU WORK ON A PAPER ROUND BY LAW? ANSWERS AT END.

- a) 2 hours a day.
- b) 4 hours a day.
- c) 6 hours a day.

People with paper rounds live close to a local shop, carry a large bag and do quite a bit of walking or cycling. The other important thing you need to have is an alarm clock, because most paper rounds are first thing in the morning before school.

You can have a paper round (or media distribution round) from the age of thirteen onwards. Lots of teenagers like the idea of a paper round. It allows you to earn some extra cash around going to school and meeting your friends. As a teenager you can expect to earn around £2.50 for a round, which will probably take about an hour. Adults also work as media distribution officers and drop leaflets through letterboxes. Adults will expect to earn the minimum wage for this, which is around £12k a year.

TWO OF THE WORST THINGS ABOUT MEDIA DISTRIBUTION ARE:

1) It is an all year round job, which isn't too bad when it's summer, but not much fun if it is pounding it down with rain or it is freezing cold.
2) The bag you have to carry can be heavy.

Q2. WHAT DO YOU THINK IS THE MAXIMUM WEIGHT A PAPER ROUND BAG CAN BE?

   a)   10kg.
   b)   15kg.
   c)   25kg?

The answer is 15 kg. It might not sound that heavy, but that is like carrying a toddler or a small suitcase on your back. Media distribution officers normally use a pushbike to speed up their round. It must be difficult to ride a bike and balance with that kind of weight on your back.

Q1 ANSWER:
A – 2 hours

Bonkers Jobs Scorecard for Media Distribution Technician

Now you've learnt about the job it's time to score it. Below we have worked out a Crazyometer score for the job – do you agree? Just mark each Aspect of the job out of 10, 1 meaning 'rubbish' and 10 meaning 'brilliant'. Then total up your score to see if you agree with the Crazyometer.

Aspect	Bonkers Jobs Score	Your Score
Are your friends impressed?	5 (Quit and spend more time with us)	
Do your parents dislike it?	4 (Not a proper job)	
Do you earn much money?	3 (More pocket money)	
Nice place to work?	3 (OK when the sun is out)	
Job opportunities increasing?	3 (Send it in an email instead)	
How brainy have you got to be?	3 (It's posting a letter!)	
Crazyometer Total Score	21	

PROTECTION SPECIALIST

WOW, WHAT A COOL JOB TITLE! This really must be an exciting job. It almost sounds a bit like a title for a movie (where some robot or strong person has to protect the world from bad guys or to be a bodyguard for a famous person).

In reality it is another case of a glamorous title for something we see advertised all the time:

INSURANCE!

Yes, a protection specialist is a stupid name for an insurance sales assistant.

Insurance is part of everyday life. It is hard to turn on the TV without seeing a Meerkat or dancing robot advertising insurance companies to protect people's cars, homes and lives in case of an accident.

Insurance sounds like the **dullest** thing on the planet, but there is lots of interesting stuff involved. Insurance isn't just about cars, houses and illnesses. You can get insurance for just about anything. Just what kind of anything, I hear you ask.

WEDDING INSURANCE – Weddings cost thousands of pounds, with the average costing around £22,000! Sometimes couples spend years planning their weddings, making sure that every detail is perfect. All this is fine, but what happens if the couple split up before their big day or if the bride or groom get cold feet and don't turn up? Well, that is why couples can now get wedding insurance, to pay for the costs of the wedding if it gets cancelled. Imagine the conversation with your partner: 'I love you and can't wait to spend the rest of my life with you, but I think we should get wedding insurance in case I change my mind!'

HOLE IN ONE INSURANCE – There is a tradition in golf that if a golfer is lucky enough to get a hole in one they have to buy everyone at the golf course a drink. Imagine the mixed feelings. On one hand you've made a 1 in 12,500 shot, on the other you might have to spend hundreds of pounds buying people you don't know a drink!

CELEBRITY BODY INSURANCE

Q1. HOW MANY OF THE BELOW ARE THOUGHT TO BE TRUE? ANSWER AT END.

- Taylor Swift's legs are insured for forty million US dollars.
- Daniel Craig's (James Bond) body is insured for 9.5 million pounds.

- Jenifer Lopez's bottom is insured for 27 million US dollars.

How cool would it be to sort out a celebrity's insurance? Also there are many fake insurance claims, so how epic would it be to bring down a fraudster and report them to the police? Some people who pay life insurance have even faked their own death so that relatives can get thousands of pounds! They would spend the rest of their life without an identity, unless of course a protection specialist busts them!

Most insurance sales assistants work in an office environment and work long hours, earning from £14k to up to £25k for experienced staff. Insurance is everywhere though, so there are good chances of becoming a protection specialist!

Q1: ANSWER:

All of them are true!

Bonkers Jobs Scorecard for Protection Specialist

Now you've learnt about the job it's time to score it. Below we have worked out a Crazyometer score for the job – do you agree? Just mark each Aspect of the job out of 10, 1 meaning 'rubbish' and 10 meaning 'brilliant'. Then total up your score to see if you agree with the Crazyometer.

Aspect	Bonkers Jobs Score	Your Score
Are your friends impressed?	5 (Boring)	
Do your parents dislike it?	5 (Sensible, urgh!)	
Do you earn much money?	5 (Average)	
Nice place to work?	5 (office all day)	
Job opportunities increasing?	6 (Everyone needs insurance)	
How brainy have you got to be?	4 (No need for university)	
Crazyometer Total Score	30	

LEARNING AND DEVELOPMENT LEAD CONSULTANT GLOBAL MARKET TRAINING, E LEARNING AND PROFESSIONAL QUALIFICATIONS

WHAT A JOB TITLE! You are probably thinking it is the longest job title in the world. Well you are right! Try saying it out loud a few times. **Impossible, isn't it?** How utterly stupid to have such a long job title? Let's not be so stupid and instead call it a **LADLCGMTELPQ!** See what words you can find using these letters:

WRITE YOUR WORDS HERE:

....

Whoever came up with the **LADLCGMTELPQ** job title must be totally bonkers. They have pretty much taken lots of big words and put them together to make them sound interesting and important! Basically a **LADLCGMTELPQ** is a finance consultant and trainer. This is someone who can advise people and companies on their accounts and financial information, and also help train up other staff that want to be financial consultants.

Working as a financial consultant and trainer you need to study quite hard and have a seriously good head for maths and numbers. There are more and more businesses starting up each day and most want expert advice on how to manage things like tax, how to increase their profits and make more money! This means than we might see more **LADLCGMTELPQ** in the future! The pay is likely to be good with earning s of £25k - £50k and the hours tend to be normal office 9-5.

Imagine if you are a **LADLCGMTELPQ** and have a half an hour business meeting with a new customer. You would spend a great deal of your time introducing yourself!

Here are some other examples of actual job titles that are far too long:

DIRECT DEBIT AND MEMBERSHIP AND PROFESSIONAL DEVELOPMENT STOCK AND CREDIT ADMINISTRATOR – Customer Services Administrator

PSYCHONEUROENDOCRINOLOGIST – This must be one of the longest words in the world, let alone job title! It is a scientific job which looks into hormones which make the brain behave in certain ways and are responsible for our moods.

TEMPORARY PART-TIME LIBRARIES NORTH WEST INTER-LIBRARY LOAN BUSINESS UNIT ADMINISTRATION ASSISTANT – in other words a library assistant!

What a complete waste of time it must be to think up these job titles. The more words that are in a job title, the more stupid the job is!

BONKERS JOBS SCORECARD FOR LEARNING AND DEVELOPMENT LEAD CONSULTANT GLOBAL MARKET TRAINING, E LEARNING AND PROFESSIONAL QUALIFICATIONS

Now you've learnt about the job it's time to score it. Below we have worked out a Crazyometer score for the job – do you agree? Just mark each Aspect of the job out of 10, 1 meaning 'rubbish' and 10 meaning 'brilliant'. Then total up your score to see if you agree with the Crazyometer.

Aspect	Bonkers Jobs Score	Your Score
Are your friends impressed?	3 (What is that?)	
Do your parents dislike it?	3 (How could they explain to their friends what job you do?)	
Do you earn much money?	7 (This is looking better)	
Nice place to work?	5 (Always inside)	
Job opportunities increasing?	6 (Oh dear)	
How brainy have you got to be?	7 (Very clever to remember your job title!)	
Crazyometer Total Score	31	

Choose Your Stupid Job

Now you've ventured into the world of stupid jobs it's time to think about which would be stupid enough for you. To do that you need to complete the table below. Just take the scores you gave each stupid job and place them in the table below.

Job	Magic Letter	Crazyometer score	Your score
Education Centre Nourishment Consultant	A	29	
Barista	S	38	
Colour Distribution Technician	R	29	
Media Distribution Officer	C	21	
Protection Specialist	E	30	
LADLCGMTELPQ	I	31	

Do you agree with the Crazyometer scoring? The good news is that the only right answer is your answer! We all see the world differently and it's your opinion that matters here.

So the stupid job you have scored the highest is:

....

There is a Magic Letter next to that job – what is it? You need to collect these magic letters. In the last chapter we will use these to help you find your own bonkers job.

Write your magic letter here:

....

YOUR CRAZY CAREER PATH

You've reached the end of *The Bonkers Book of Jobs*. You now know what they don't tell you at school.

But your career path is only just starting. Do you know what you want to do yet?

Maybe you've decided that it's to be the prime minister. Or perhaps worked out that portable toilet service deliverer is not for you?

To help you decide, enter below the job you have chosen from each chapter and then next to it enter the crazy career path magic letter:

Chapter	Jobs I have chosen is	My magic letter is
Disgusting jobs		
Weird jobs		
Scary jobs		
Cool jobs		
Delicious jobs		
Stupid jobs		

Now here's the magic bit.
Total up your letters.
The letter(s) you have the most: ....

Now carry on reading and the magic letter will tell you which bonkers career path you might take in the future.

Below we have listed jobs that match your magic letter. Have a look. Which job do you want to do in the future?

Are you A?

If so, you are *artistic*: You have a good imagination and you like to be creative. You tend to be quite outgoing and possibly dramatic.

OUR BONKERS ARTISTIC JOBS ARE:
Artist, comedian, fashion designer, cake decorator, mascot and education centre nourishment consultant.

Did you know that other *artistic* jobs include: architect, musician, photographer, actor and interior designer?

Our Crazyometer makes **COMEDIAN** the craziest of all the *artistic* jobs with a score of **39**.

Are you C?

If so, you are **conventional**: You like careful

planning and things doing in a certain way. You may also prefer a routine and are happy to follow rules.

OUR BONKERS CONVENTIONAL JOBS ARE:
Health and safety inspector, waste recycling officer, accountant, dog food taster, dice inspector and media distribution technician.

Did you know that other **conventional** jobs include: pharmacist, maths teacher, carpenter, librarian and human resources?

Our Crazyometer makes **DICE INSPECTOR** the craziest of all the **conventional** jobs with a score of **41**.

Are you E?

If so, you are **enterprising**: You are good at persuading and managing people. You are quite ambitious and confident and could sell anything to anyone!

Our Bonkers **enterprising** jobs are: maggot farmer, prime minister, entrepreneur, restaurant owner, golf ball diver and protection specialist.

Did you know that other **enterprising** jobs include: sales, journalist, fundraiser, customer service and buyer.

Our Crazyometer makes **MAGGOT FARMER** the craziest of all the **enterprising** jobs with a score of **38**.

Are you I?

If so, you are **investigative**: You like to solve problems, mathematical equations or scientific experiments.

Our Bonkers **investigative** jobs are portable toilet service deliverer, bomb disposal expert, Antarctic researcher, genetic engineer, face feeler and LADLCGMTELPQ.

Did you know that other **investigative** jobs include: surgeons, chemists, engineers, detectives and counsellors?

Our Crazyometer makes **GENETIC ENGINEER** the craziest of all the **investigative** jobs with a score of **43**.

Are you R?

If so you are **realistic**: You like to make or do things and have practical skills or strength and stamina.

Our Bonkers **realistic** jobs are abattoir worker, stunt

person, game designer, cheese maker, Lego sculptor and colour distribution technician.

Did you know that other **realistic** jobs include: agriculture, military, personal trainer, driver, environmental science?

Our Crazyometer makes **GAME DESIGNER** the craziest of all the **realistic** jobs with a score of **42.**

Are you S?

If so, you are **social**: You have a genuine interest in people and like to help others. You are friendly, outgoing and understanding.

Our Bonkers **social** jobs are: beautician, police officer, mobile ice cream seller, dietician, dog yoga instructor and barista.

Did you know that other **social** jobs include: clergy, teacher, psychologist, social worker, hotel rep.

Our Crazyometer makes **BARISTA** the craziest of all the **social** jobs with a score of **38.**

Now you have matched yourself with a load of jobs, what do you think about them?

Why not ask a friend or your family? What letter do they think describes you the best? How about them? What letter do you think describes them best?

REMEMBER! – people can expect to have nine different jobs in their lifetime – so there's plenty of time to find the Bonkers Job that suits you.